U.S. Department of Justice
Office of Justice Programs
National Institute of Justice

I0476837

National Institute of Justice

Law Enforcement and Corrections Standards and Testing Program

Guide to the Technologies of Concealed Weapon and Contraband Imaging and Detection

NIJ Guide 602–00

ABOUT THE LAW ENFORCEMENT AND CORRECTIONS STANDARDS AND TESTING PROGRAM

The Law Enforcement and Corrections Standards and Testing Program is sponsored by the Office of Science and Technology of the National Institute of Justice (NIJ), U.S. Department of Justice. The program responds to the mandate of the Justice System Improvement Act of 1979, which directed NIJ to encourage research and development to improve the criminal justice system and to disseminate the results to Federal, State, and local agencies.

The Law Enforcement and Corrections Standards and Testing Program is an applied research effort that determines the technological needs of justice system agencies, sets minimum performance standards for specific devices, tests commercially available equipment against those standards, and disseminates the standards and the test results to criminal justice agencies nationally and internationally.

The program operates through:

The *Law Enforcement and Corrections Technology Advisory Council* (LECTAC), consisting of nationally recognized criminal justice practitioners from Federal, State, and local agencies, which assesses technological needs and sets priorities for research programs and items to be evaluated and tested.

The *Office of Law Enforcement Standards* (OLES) at the National Institute of Standards and Technology, which develops voluntary national performance standards for compliance testing to ensure that individual items of equipment are suitable for use by criminal justice agencies. The standards are based upon laboratory testing and evaluation of representative samples of each item of equipment to determine the key attributes, develop test methods, and establish minimum performance requirements for each essential attribute. In addition to the highly technical standards, OLES also produces technical reports and user guidelines that explain in nontechnical terms the capabilities of available equipment.

The *National Law Enforcement and Corrections Technology Center (NLECTC),* operated by a grantee, which supervises a national compliance testing program conducted by independent laboratories. The standards developed by OLES serve as performance benchmarks against which commercial equipment is measured. The facilities, personnel, and testing capabilities of the independent laboratories are evaluated by OLES prior to testing each item of equipment, and OLES helps the NLECTC staff review and analyze data. Test results are published in Equipment Performance Reports designed to help justice system procurement officials make informed purchasing decisions.

Publications are available at no charge through the National Law Enforcement and Corrections Technology Center. Some documents are also available online through the Internet/World Wide Web. To request a document or additional information, call 800–248–2742 or 301–519–5060, or write:

National Law Enforcement and Corrections Technology Center
P.O. Box 1160
Rockville, MD 20849–1160
E-Mail: *asknlectc@nlectc.org*
World Wide Web address: *http://www.nlectc.org*

The National Institute of Justice is a component of the Office of Justice Programs, which also includes the Bureau of Justice Assistance, the Bureau of Justice Statistics, the Office of Juvenile Justice and Delinquency Prevention, and the Office for Victims of Crime.

U.S. Department of Justice
Office of Justice Programs
National Institute of Justice

Guide to the Technologies of Concealed Weapon and Contraband Imaging and Detection

NIJ Guide 602–00

Nicholas G. Paulter
Electricity Division
National Institute of Standards and Technology
Gaithersburg, MD 20899

Prepared for:
National Institute of Justice
Office of Science and Technology
Washington, DC 20531

February 2001

NCJ 184432

National Institute of Justice

Julie E. Samuels
Acting Director

The technical effort to develop this guide was conducted
under Interagency Agreement 94–IJ–R–004
Project No. 97–012–CTT.

This guide was prepared by the Office of Law Enforcement
Standards (OLES) of the National Institute of Standards
and Technology (NIST) under the direction of
A. George Lieberman, Program Manager, Detection,
Inspection and Enforcement Technologies, and
Kathleen M. Higgins, Director of OLES.
The work resulting from this guide was sponsored by the
National Institute of Justice, Dr. David G. Boyd, Director,
Office of Science and Technology.

FOREWORD

The Office of Law Enforcement Standards (OLES) of the National Institute of Standards and Technology (NIST) furnishes technical support to the National Institute of Justice (NIJ) program to strengthen law enforcement and criminal justice in the United States. OLES's function is to conduct research that will assist law enforcement and criminal justice agencies in the selection and procurement of quality equipment.

OLES is: (1) subjecting existing equipment to laboratory testing and evaluation, and (2) conducting research leading to the development of several series of documents, including national standards, user guides, and technical reports.

This document covers research conducted by OLES under the sponsorship of the National Institute of Justice. Additional reports as well as other documents are being issued under the OLES program in the areas of protective clothing and equipment, communications systems, emergency equipment, investigative aids, security systems, vehicles, weapons, and analytical techniques and standard reference materials used by the forensic community.

Technical comments and suggestions concerning this guide are invited from all interested parties. They may be addressed to the Director, Office of Law Enforcement Standards, National Institute of Standards and Technology, Gaithersburg, MD 20899–8102.

Dr. David G. Boyd, Director
Office of Science and Technology
National Institute of Justice

BACKGROUND

The Office of Law Enforcement Standards (OLES) was established by the National Institute of Justice (NIJ) to provide focus on two major objectives: (1) to find existing equipment that can be purchased today, and (2) to develop new law-enforcement equipment that can be made available as soon as possible. A part of OLES's mission is to become thoroughly familiar with existing equipment, to evaluate its performance by means of objective laboratory tests, to develop and improve these methods of test, to develop performance standards for selected equipment items, and to prepare guidelines for the selection and use of this equipment. All of these activities are directed toward providing law enforcement agencies with assistance in making good equipment selections and acquisitions in accordance with their own requirements.

As the OLES program has matured, there has been a gradual shift in the objectives of the OLES projects. The initial emphasis on the development of standards has decreased, and the emphasis on the development of guidelines has increased. For the significance of this shift in emphasis to be appreciated, the precise definitions of the words "standard" and "guideline" as used in this context must be clearly understood.

A "standard" for a particular item of equipment is understood to be a formal document, in a conventional format, that details the performance that the equipment is required to give, and describes test methods by which its actual performance can be measured. These requirements are technical, and are stated in terms directly related to the equipment's use. The basic purposes of a standard are (1) to be a reference in procurement documents created by purchasing officers who wish to specify equipment of the "standard" quality, and (2) to identify objectively equipment of acceptable performance.

Note that a standard is not intended to inform and guide the reader; that is the function of a "guideline." Guidelines are written in non-technical language and are addressed to the potential user of the equipment. They include a general discussion of the equipment, its important performance attributes, the various models currently on the market, objective test data where available, and any other information that might help the reader make a rational selection among the various options or alternatives available to him or her.

> *A standard is not intended to inform and guide the reader; that is the function of a guideline*

This guide is provided to describe to the reader the technology used in hand-held and walk-through metal detectors that is pertinent for use in weapon and contraband detection.

Kathleen Higgins
National Institute of Standards and Technology
February 2001

ACKNOWLEDGMENTS

This document addresses the requirements and concerns expressed by representatives from the law enforcement and corrections (LEC) community regarding concealed weapon and contraband imaging and detection. These requirements and concerns were obtained from interviews with local, State, and Federal LEC agencies. In particular, the following local and State LEC agencies have provided inputs useful to the preparation of this document:

Allen County Sheriff's Department, Fort Wayne, IN
Arapahoe County Sheriff's Department, Littleton, CO
Buffalo Police Department, Buffalo, NY
California Department of Corrections, Sacramento, CA
Erie County Sheriff's Department, Erie County, NY
Fairfax County Sheriff's Department, Fairfax, VA
Frederick County Adult Detention Center, Frederick, MD
Los Angeles County Sheriff's Department, Monterey Park, CA
Montgomery County Police, Rockville, MD
New York State Department of Corrections, Buffalo, NY
New Hampshire Department of Corrections, Concord, NH
Rhode Island Department of Corrections, Cranston, RI
Rome Police Department, Rome, NY

The following Federal LEC agencies have also provided useful comments and contributions:

Bureau of Alcohol, Tobacco, and Firearms, U.S. Department of Treasury
Bureau of Diplomatic Security, U.S. Department of State
Federal Aviation Administration, U.S. Department of Transportation
Federal Bureau of Investigation, U.S. Department of Justice
Federal Bureau of Prisons, U.S. Department of Justice
United States Secret Service, U.S. Department of Treasury

Others have contributed to the development of this document: M. Misakian of the National Institute of Standards and Technology (NIST), Gaithersburg, MD and G.A. Lieberman of the Office of Law Enforcement Standards (OLES) of NIST furnished technical comments and suggestions; J.L. Tierney and D.A. Abrahamson, both under contract with NIST during preparation of this document, provided technical and editorial comments and recommendations; and S.E. Lyles of OLES and B.A. Bell of NIST provided editorial and administrative support.

CONTENTS

FIGURES

TABLES

COMMONLY USED SYMBOLS AND ABBREVIATIONS

A	ampere	H	henry	nm	nanometer
ac	alternating current	h	hour	No.	number
AM	amplitude modulation	hf	high frequency	o.d.	outside diameter
cd	candela	Hz	hertz (c/s)	O	ohm
cm	centimeter	i.d.	inside diameter	p.	page
CP	chemically pure	in	inch	Pa	pascal
c/s	cycle per second	IR	infrared	pe	probable error
d	day	J	joule	pp.	pages
dB	decibel	L	lambert	ppm	parts per million
dc	direct current	L	liter	qt	quart
•C	degree Celsius	lb	pound	rad	radian
•F	degree Fahrenheit	lbf	pound-force	rf	radio frequency
dia	diameter	lbf•in	pound-force inch	rh	relative humidity
emf	electromotive force	lm	lumen	s	second
eq	equation	ln	logarithm (base e)	SD	standard deviation
F	farad	log	logarithm (base 10)	sec.	section
fc	footcandle	M	molar	SWR	standing wave ratio
fig.	figure	m	meter	uhf	ultrahigh frequency
FM	frequency modulation	min	minute	UV	ultraviolet
ft	foot	mm	millimeter	V	volt
ft/s	foot per second	mph	miles per hour	vhf	very high frequency
g	acceleration	m/s	meter per second	W	watt
g	gram	N	newton	?	wavelength
gr	grain	N•m	newton meter	wt	weight

area=unit^2 (e.g., ft^2, in^2, etc.); volume=unit^3 (e.g., ft^3, m^3, etc.)

PREFIXES

d	deci (10^{-1})	da	deka (10)
c	centi (10^{-2})	h	hecto (10^2)
m	milli (10^{-3})	k	kilo (10^3)
μ	micro (10^{-6})	M	mega (10^6)
n	nano (10^{-9})	G	giga (10^9)
p	pico (10^{-12})	T	tera (10^{12})

COMMON CONVERSIONS (See ASTM E380)

0.30480 m = 1 ft	4.448222 N = 1 lbf
2.54 cm = 1 in	1.355818 J = 1 ft•lbf
0.4535924 kg = 1 lb	0.1129848 N•m = 1 lbf•in
0.06479891g = 1 gr	14.59390 N/m = 1 lbf/ft
0.9463529 L = 1 qt	6894.757 Pa = 1 lbf/in^2
3600000 J = 1 kW•hr	1.609344 km/h = 1 mph

Temperature: $T_{•C} = (T_{•F} • 32) \times 5/9$

Temperature: $T_{•F} = (T_{•C} \times 9/5) + 32$

1. INTRODUCTION

A concealed weapon and contraband imaging and detection system (CWCIDS) is an instrument, a device, or equipment designed to find items considered to be weapons or contraband.[1]   A weapon is any object that can do harm to another individual or group of individuals. This definition not only includes objects typically thought of as weapons, such as knives and firearms, but also explosives, chemicals, etc. Contraband items include illegal drugs and any other item that is controlled or forbidden by a particular law enforcement or corrections agency. Consequently, contraband may include tobacco, any metallic object that can be used to defeat security constraints, drug paraphernalia, etc.

There are a variety of different technologies either being used or developed for CWCIDS applications, such as x-ray imaging, microwave holography, acoustic detection, etc. These CWCIDSs may be utilized in a variety of forms including the following: hand-held close-proximity scanning; stationary-positioned, walk-by scanning; hand-held, stand-off scanning; etc. Which of the forms used is limited by the given CWCIDS technology. For example, present technology precludes x-ray imaging from being using in a hand-held stand-off scanning device. The law enforcement and corrections officer may apply these CWCIDSs in various environments (indoor and outdoor, controlled and uncontrolled areas, day and night, etc.) and for various scenarios (pat-down search, surveillance, tracking, etc.).

1.1 Purpose of Guide

The purpose of the Guide is to provide information that will help members of the law enforcement and corrections community, who are present or potential users and operators of CWCIDSs, better understand the operation, limitations, and applicability of CWCIDS technology to their specific application and to provide an overview of the state of development in the CWCIDS for the mutual benefit of all interested parties. Some of the CWCIDSs are still under development and are included here for completeness. This Guide focuses on CWCIDSs that are intended for use on humans; that is, for detection of contraband and weapons concealed on human bodies. Accordingly, this Guide contains a technical review and discussion only of the various technologies that are being used or developed for concealed weapon and contraband imaging and detection on humans. A discussion of the limitations of these systems is provided, as are potential applications and general application-specific considerations. This discussion is also limited to the CWCIDS that use electromagnetic or acoustic phenomena for detection.

The target audience for this Guide is technical lay people. This Guide is not intended to provide a complete technical discourse on the theory of operation of any of the different systems that are described herein. However, references to literature that contain technical detail are provided for those

---

[1]Important concepts will appear in bolded text.

1

that are interested in more information. Furthermore, this document is not intended to describe, discuss, or endorse one particular company's CWCIDS-based implementation of a given technology. However, in many situations only one manufacturer is using a particular technology for a CWCIDS and the discussion naturally follows that manufacturer's implementation.

1.2 Layout of Guide

The Guide contains a brief tutorial on science topics that are necessary to understand and compare various CWCIDSs and, possibly, on how to apply these systems for a specific application. Sections 2, 3, 4, 5, and 6 of the Guide are written so that the more deeply nested or embedded are the subsections, the more technical is the information contained in that subsection. For example, the text immediately following a section labeled with a single numeric section designation (3.1, 3.2, 3.3, etc.) is very basic or introductory. On the other hand, the text in a section labeled with a five numeric section designation (3.1.2.3.1, 3.2.1.2.2, etc.) will contain the most technical information. However, it is hoped that even the most technical information is presented at a level that can be easily understood. A brief discussion of radiation-exposure safety issues is also given in section 6. Section 7 of the Guide contains descriptions of the technology presently being used or under development for CWCIDSs. In section 8, suggestions and recommendations are given for performance standards. These suggested performance standards can also be used for procurement purposes.

The CWCIDSs can be implemented in a variety of ways, and these are described in this Guide along with possible applications. These different implementations will be distinguished, in this document, by the type of information that is provided by the system (see sec. 3) and how the system is deployed (sec. 4). Furthermore, CWCIDSs can be further differentiated on whether active or passive illumination or black-body emission is used (see sec. 5). In addition to these topics, there are a variety of other issues (such as cost, ease of use, etc.) that the law enforcement and corrections agencies have to consider when deciding upon a particular CWCIDS for its particular application. This Guide is also an attempt to address these issues.

2. POSSIBLE APPLICATIONS

In this section, potential applications for CWCIDSs are briefly described and considerations are given to some important factors that may help in deciding which CWCIDS is optimal for a given application. For certain of these applications, the CWCIDS may be very simple and small, such as a hand-held metal detector, and in other cases the CWCIDS may be very complex or large, like a remote radar imaging system or magnetic resonance imaging (MRI) system. The applications described are intended as examples of how CWCIDSs may be used and are not intended to limit more creative usage.

2.1 Detection

Detection of a concealed weapon or contraband is the most basic CWCIDS function or application. **Detection gives the operator information on the presence of objects in the detection space.** The detection space is the volume over which the CWCIDS operator is searching (see sec. 3). The operator, however, does not know what type of object is detected when using a detection-only CWCIDS, only that something was detected. The detected object may not even be hidden. For example, conventional walk-through metal detectors will let the operator know that metal objects have passed through the portal, but these systems do not pinpoint the location of the metal objects (although some walk-through systems provide zoned detection). And, unless the magnitude of the indication is dependent on the mass of the metal passing through the portal, the operator will not know the size of the object. Because detection is the simplest type of CWCIDS application, a detection-only CWCIDS should be the least expensive and easiest to maintain of all types of CWCIDSs. But, as already mentioned, a detection-only CWCIDS provides the least amount of information.

2.1.1 Imaging-Based Detection

Another type of detection-only CWCIDS, albeit much more sophisticated than that just described, is a CWCIDS that acquires images of the detection space and then uses image recognition to convert the image into an indication (such as an audible or visual alarm). The imaging and image recognition capability would make such a detection-only CWCIDS very complicated and much more expensive than a simple detection-only type system. Moreover, the image recognition function of this type of detection-only CWCIDS would require access to or have a large information (data) storage capability (see sec. 2.1.2).

Image recognition usually requires large computing power and does not at present provide real-time detection capability. Therefore, based on present technology, this type of CWCIDS could not be used to find contraband hidden on individuals in a line of moving people unless sufficient computing power is available.

3

2.1.2 Image Recognition Requirements

For the computer to recognize a specific weapon or threat item, the computer will have to compare the threat item with an electronic catalog of images of uniquely-shaped threat items, and this includes images for all possible unique orientations for each unique threat item. Only catalogued images of uniquely-shaped threat items are required for comparison because no new information is obtained if a catalogued image is only a scaled replica of another catalogued image. Unique orientations, on the other hand, are important because a weapon may have a significantly different appearance if viewed from the sides, the top, etc. For example, consider the appearance of a handgun viewed from different angles. A handgun looks significantly different if viewed from the side or down the bore of the barrel. The apparent (or observed) uniqueness of a threat item based on its orientation, however, will also depend on the image resolution of the CWCIDS: the less resolution in the image, the less likely the unique orientations will appear different. As an example of the effect of resolution on the uniqueness of appearance of a threat item, again consider a handgun, specifically, consider viewing a handgun with an unaided eye. Standing one foot away from a handgun, one would realize that each orientation of the handgun gives a very unique visual image. Standing a hundred yards away, one may be able to differentiate between front (down the bore), side, and top views, but one probably could not visually distinguish between front and back views. The front and back views may appear to be just a block of metal. In image recognition, the more ambiguous the image, the more likely the imaging-based detection-only CWCIDS will fail to recognize a threat object or be fraught with false alarms.

2.2 Imaging

Imaging CWCIDSs are much more complicated than detection-only systems. **An imaging-type CWCIDS will include a detector or detector array (see sec. 3.1) and/or a scanning system, image acquisition hardware and software, display hardware, etc.** However, the information provided can be much more useful than a detection-only CWCIDS. How useful the image information is will depend on the clarity of the image. For example, if the image is very difficult to decipher and/or requires a highly-trained operator to interpret the images, the system will not be practical to most LEC agencies because of budgetary and manpower constraints. Most imaging-type CWCIDSs, at the time of this writing, do not produce real-time images but require, at a minimum, a few seconds to generate an image. Therefore, an imaging-type CWCIDS may be a bottleneck in a high-throughput security checkpoint and should not be used as a primary screening tool in such a situation. On the other hand, if the imaging system produces high-clarity images, then this imaging system may reduce the actual time required for secondary screening. A very good example of a concealed object imaging system that exhibits high image clarity is the cabinet x-ray system used at airports to screen carry-on luggage.

Based on present technology, imaging would be used where throughput is not an issue, such as secondary screening at security checkpoints. Furthermore, depending on the technology used to obtain an image, imaging may be further restricted because of privacy issues. For example, there exist some imaging-type CWCIDSs, such as some x-ray imaging systems, that provide detailed images of anatomical features. In most situations, displaying detailed anatomical features of a person is a violation of that individual's privacy. Moreover, there may be privacy concerns simply to acquire data that can provide images with anatomical detail even though an image is never displayed or if the CWCIDS is incapable of displaying the image.

Imaging-type CWCIDSs will be more expensive than detection-only CWCIDSs and may not be as rugged. Typically, the imaging-type CWCIDS will be larger than the detection-only CWCIDSs, have greater power requirements, and be more difficult and costly to maintain.

2.3 Locating

A locating-type CWCIDS is used to show the operator where a contraband item is hidden within the detection space of the CWCIDS. Locating an object in the detection space facilitates confiscation from, or further examination of, the person with the concealed object. Although locating the contraband item does not require an image, an imaging-type CWCIDS can be used to locate objects in the detection space. The simplest locating-type CWCIDSs presently available consists of a group of noninteracting detectors, such as zoned walk-through metal detectors. However, in these walk-through detectors, only coarse positional information of the metal object is provided. In these zoned walk-through systems, the detectors are arranged vertically along the columns of the portal. Nonwalk-through locating-type CWCIDSs could also be designed to use the same technology as that used for through-the-wall people detection and location. However, the spatial resolution of present through-the-wall person finders is not adequate for a CWCIDS.

Locating an object, in terms of CWCIDS cost and complexity, is closer to a detection-only CWCIDS than to an imaging-type CWCIDS. Because the locating-type CWCIDS will likely contain a group of detectors, acquisition of information would be rapid. Since imaging is not required, the locating-type CWCIDS would be simpler to operate, lower in cost, and easier to maintain than an imaging-type CWCIDS.

2.4 Monitoring and Surveillance

A monitoring- or surveillance-type CWCIDS provides remote detection capability and, therefore, requires additional hardware and software required for that purpose. Monitoring and surveillance imply a "hands-off" operation where a remotely located operator is warned, by the monitoring-type CWCIDS, of the presence of the contraband item in the area being controlled or monitored. Accordingly, the monitoring-type CWCIDS must provide a remote interface capability and possibly information storage. A non-CWCIDS example of monitoring is the ubiquitous closed-circuit television camera. The detection function of a monitoring-type CWCIDS could be provided by either of the basic CWCIDSs: imaging-type or detection-only. The selection of which basic CWCIDS to use would depend on the detail required for the monitoring application. For example, if the area is monitored for the presence of metal objects or certain chemicals, a detection-only CWCIDS would be satisfactory. For these cases, however, a means for distinguishing between innocuous items and the targeted contraband items must be provided because of the potential for false alarms. On the other hand, if the LEC officer wishes to identify objects in the detection space, then a more sophisticated imaging-type CWCIDS would be required. In this case, image recognition capability and information storage would be required (see sec. 2.1.2). Having the ability to store and compare image information would also allow a monitoring-type CWCIDS to perform frame-to-frame comparisons, thereby providing a means of monitoring the movement of unauthorized items within the detection space.

A surveillance or monitoring application may also be performed in an uncontrolled environment, where the detection space may not be constant, or where relocation of the CWCIDS is required. A monitoring-type CWCIDS, therefore, must accommodate variable temperatures, exposure to environmental extremes (rain, snow, blowing sand, etc.), frequent movement, and relocation. If monitoring is performed in controlled areas, such as in buildings or parking areas and, therefore, has a specific detection space to examine, the CWCIDS may be housed within a controlled-environment enclosure to ameliorate the effects of changing environmental conditions.

A monitoring-type CWCIDS may also be used to acquire information from a large area (such as around the corner of a building, up and down a street, etc.) and, thus, would require scanning capability or the use of several sensor arrays. The scanning could be done either mechanically or electronically depending on the specific technology used. Because the monitoring-type CWCIDS may be used to gather data on a large area, it must be designed to accommodate a variety of possible backgrounds and still provide a consistent image or indication to the operator. That is, regardless of where the CWCIDS is directed or the conditions of operation, the information obtained must be automatically adjusted so that a specific object when detected or viewed from all possible directions and under all possible conditions will give the operator the same relative information. This is similar to adjusting a camera for various light conditions.

The additional requirements of the monitoring-type CWCIDS, relative to the imaging-type or detection-only CWCIDS, will necessitate additional software and hardware. Therefore, the costs and complexity would be greater for a monitoring-type CWCIDS than for a detection-only or imaging-type CWCIDS. Nevertheless, since one person could operate multiple monitoring-type CWCIDSs, an agency may have an overall cost savings when monitoring with CWCIDSs. The monitoring-type CWCIDS must have an adequate response time because monitoring will require immediate (less than a second) information transfer to the operator so that the operator can take appropriate action.

2.5 Tracking

Tracking is the process of following or retracing the movements of a targeted item (or items) over time. A tracking-type CWCIDS, therefore, will provide the operator with information on the whereabouts of a target item. The tracking-type CWCIDS uses either an imaging-type or detection-only CWCIDS for basic object identification; which basic CWCIDS is used will depend on the detail required to identify an object. In addition, the tracking-type CWCIDS will have the ability to map (such as with triangulation) the movements of the identified object over time. Tracking can be performed automatically or by an operator. In either case, the more detail contained in the acquired information, the easier it will be to follow the object. For automatic tracking systems, where the tracking data will be stored electronically, additional detail on the object will prevent tracking innocuous items. If the tracking–type CWCIDS is operated by an officer, a detection-only CWCIDS is sufficient because the officer/operator is able to interpret the information provided by the CWCIDS. Tracking will demand that the tracking-type CWCIDS be transportable and, therefore, fairly light weight, battery powered, and capable of withstanding bumping, exposure to spilled liquids, etc.

A tracking-type CWCIDS would be less complicated and costly than a surveillance-type CWCIDS and probably will be around the same cost and complexity as a monitoring-type CWCIDS. If tracking a specific item is required, which would necessitate an image-type CWCIDS component, the imaging system will have to be fast enough to provide sufficient detail to map the positions of the items. Furthermore, depending on the space to be scrutinized, the tracking CWCIDS may require some sort of scanning system. A tracking-type CWCIDS may be used in a variety of environmental conditions and, so, should be tolerant to environmental extremes.

3. TYPE OF INFORMATION OBTAINED

The CWCIDS can also be classified by the type of information that is provided or presented to the operator. This classification is based on the number of dimensions contained in the information. The information provided by the CWCIDS can be in zero-dimensional (0D), 1D, 2D, or 3D. The easiest way to understand this classification scheme is to make comparisons to geometric objects. In geometry, a point is a 0D object, a line is a 1D object, a plane (flat surface) is a 2D object, and a nonflat surface or a volume is a 3D object.

Examples of 0D information from a CWCIDS are the audible and visual alarms from hand-held metal weapon detectors. With 0D information, all you know is that an object exists at an unspecified location within the detection space of the CWCIDS; the operator does not know if the item is a contraband item. The operator may know the size of the object if the alarm is proportional to the mass of the object. Examples of 1D information from CWCIDS are the vertical light-emitting diode (LED) display of some zoned walk-through metal weapon detectors. Although the zones are relatively large, it does provide some coarse information on the vertical distribution of metal objects within the portal region of the walk-through metal detector. The 2D information is more common in CWCIDSs and in our everyday lives. All pictures are 2D information. Similarly, the planar images (like a photograph) from thermal and millimeter-wave imaging systems are examples of 2D information. Pictures and photographs do not contain 3D information even though we can infer the approximate location or displacement of one object in the photograph relative to another object. We can make these inferences on distances because we are familiar with the sizes of the objects in the photograph. If we look at photographs of an un-manned scientific research vehicle on the surface of the moon, we may mistake both the sizes of lunar objects and their distances because of our expectation of the size of the research vehicle. Pictures may also contain visual cues, such as shading, scales, legends, etc., to help determine size and location of objects in a picture. Some zoned walk-through metal detectors not only show vertical location but also lateral location. The vertical and lateral information provides a very coarse 2D image. An example of 3D information is the volume images provided by radar-based through-the-wall people imaging and ranging systems. The distinction between 3D and 2D images is that 3D information includes range (distance) information.

For all these different CWCIDSs, however, the detection space for which data is obtained is a volume (3D space). In figure 1, the 2-D image of an object in the target space is depicted. The area between the dashed lines is the detection space. If an object falls partially outside of the detection space, then the image will be clipped (as shown in fig. 1). In figure 2, the same detection space is examined by a 0D-type CWCIDS and, as shown, provides only an indication of the presence of the object and not any information on the distribution of objects within its detection space. The "idiot lights" or meters (ammeter, oil meter, etc.) on automobile dashboards are examples of 0D information; they provide the least amount of information to the operator. The "idiot light" warns if an extreme condition has occurred for some parameter (such as temperature, oil pressure, etc.) and the meter indicates the magnitude (or size) of that parameter. However, in neither case does the operator know how that

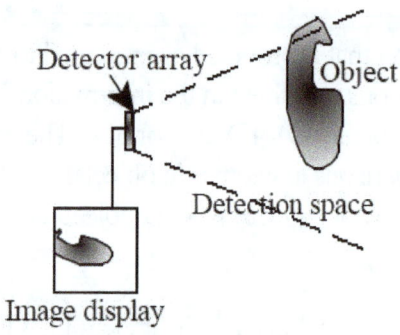 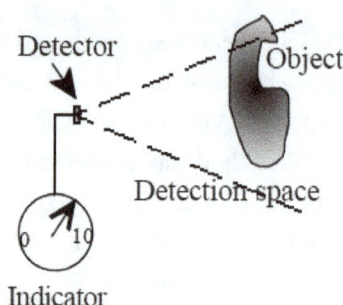

Figure 1. Image of an object that is in the detection space

Figure 2. Indication of the presence of an object that is in the detection space

parameter varies throughout appropriate parts of the motor. It is very important to distinguish between an image and an indication because most CWCIDS supply either image or indication information. Sections 3.1 and 3.2 contain additional discussion and examples to clarify the distinction between an imager and an indicator. Even those CWCIDS that provide 1D or 3D information can be described as providing either multiple indications or multiple images. For example, the 3D information obtained from the through-the-wall people finders can be considered to be multiple layered 2D images where the separation between layered images is known. Similarly, the zoned walk-through metal detectors actually use a vertically-arranged set of sources and detectors where each pair of sources and detectors provides 0D information. However, the distinction between an imager and an indicator is not necessarily the number of detectors.

3.1 Imagers and Indicators

Both imagers and indicators contain one or more detectors. Typically, a system that provides an indication will contain only one detector whereas an imaging system may contain many detectors, which is called a detector array. A detector array may contain thousands of individual detectors, such as the detector arrays used in camcorders. An imager may also use only one detector. In the case where the imager uses only one detector, the image is formed by scanning the detection space of the detector over the detection space of the image. The scanning can be done mechanically or electronically depending on overall system cost, ruggedness, and other requirements. Conversely, an imaging system can be used as an indicator by utilizing image recognition hardware and/or software without displaying the image (see sec. 2.1.1).

Reduction of an image to an indication (such as an audible alarm) may be used or desired in situations where the image is difficult to interpret by an operator, where the imager is being used in an unstaffed

10

operation, or when the image may contain sensitive information. Reduction of an image to an indication requires that some part of the image be recognized by the CWCIDS and then interpreted as a threat or contraband object; this requires image recognition capability.

3.2 Example of an Indication and an Image

The following example will help clarify the difference between an image and an indication. Consider a glass wall with opaque (nontransparent) pieces of paper stuck to it; the paper blocks half of the transmitted light and can be removed from or moved around on the glass wall (see fig. 3). In figure 3, a light is located behind the glass wall. If you were to take a picture of the wall, you would get a representation of the paper attached to the wall at the time the picture was taken: this is an image, or 2D information. A light meter, on the other hand, will give a reading (an indication) of the amount of light passing through the wall; this is 0D information. With the indicator, you could tell how much of the wall is covered by the opaque paper from the magnitude of the indication. However, you would not know how the paper is arranged on the wall. Both walls in figure 3 will give the same indication because in both situations half of the wall is covered with paper, and half the light is blocked.

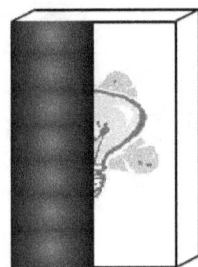 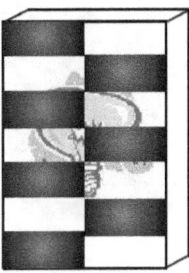

Figure 3. Two different arrangements of colored paper on a glass plate that give two different images but transmit the same amount of light energy

4. FORM FACTORS

Form factors are design variables that are related to how a human operator will use a CWCIDS. Form factors affect not only the design of a CWCIDS, but also the choice of which detection technology is used. The form factors that are considered here include the proximity of the CWCIDS to the detection space (sec. 4.1) and how portable is the CWCIDS (secs. 4.2 and 4.3). To help show how these form factors affect the application of a CWCIDS, a summary table is given in section 4.4.

4.1 Proximity

CWCIDSs fall into two general categories: those that require close proximity use and those where the operator can and must be a minimum distance from the target area. Examples of close-proximity devices include the hand-held and walk-through metal detectors, x-ray systems, and magnetic resonance imaging (MRI) systems that are being developed to look into body cavities. Stand-off devices, on the other hand, obtain information on a detection space when the target and operator are separated. Some stand-off devices require a minimum distance between the operator and the target. Examples of stand-off devices are police radar guns, infrared imagers, and cameras. For CWCIDS applications, close or near proximity will imply being within an arm's reach (approximately 1 m) and stand-off or far proximity use will imply greater than 1 m between the CWCIDS and the target.

4.2 Motion

For the context of this Guide, mobility describes the degree to which the CWCIDS may be moved during operation. That is, will the CWCIDS require stationary-use or will it be expected to operate correctly while under motion. A hand-held metal detector requires that it be moved during the search for concealed metal objects. A walk-though metal detector on the other hand will not operate properly if it is in motion. Most indicator-type hand-held CWCIDSs require movement for normal operation or are tolerant to movement. Imaging-type CWCIDSs typically will not perform well if they are under motion. However, if the motion is provided by a computer-controlled robotic mechanism, and software is available to adjust the image for movement by the robot, then the imaging-type CWCIDS will perform normally during motion.

4.3 Portability/Transportability

Portability describes how easily a system can be picked up and moved. Some CWCIDSs are permanently installed at a location whereas others are handheld and can be moved anywhere: these two examples are the extremes of portability. Portable devices typically operate on battery (dc) power whereas stationary devices typically require line (ac) power. Also, the cooling requirements of stationary systems may be more demanding than hand-held devices, such as requiring cooling fans or water. Furthermore, the environmental conditions for fixed-site systems are usually better controlled

13

than those for hand-held devices because fixed-site CWCIDSs are typically located indoors. Examples of hand-held portable systems include the hand-held metal detectors and police radar. (The radar guns are stand-off devices and the hand-held detectors are close-proximity devices.) Walk-through metal detectors, on the other hand, are stationary-use transportable walk-through systems. In this context, transportable means that the system is relocatable and can be easily shipped if necessary. Some manufacturers produce stationary-use portable walk-through metal detector systems that can be packed up in a box and transported by a personal vehicle. An MRI system is an example of a close-proximity, stationary-use, fixed-site system.

4.4 Form Factor Example Chart

The examples of CWCIDSs for given form factors are shown below in italics.

Close-proximity
   Moving
      Hand-held . . . . *wand-type metal detector*
   Stationary-use
      Portable
         Walk-through . . . . *portal-type ferromagnetic metal detector*
      Transportable
         Walk-through . . . . *portal-type metal detector*
         Walk-by, stand-by . . . . *x-ray imager*
      Fixed-site . . . . *Magnetic Resonance Imaging (MRI)*
Stand-off
   Moving
      Hand-held . . . . . *radar metal detector, acoustic hard object detector, infrared imager*
      Car-carried . . . . *gradiometer metal locator*
   Stationary-use
      Transportable . . . . *microwave radar imager*

5. PARAMETERS AFFECTING DETECTION

A CWCIDS collects data about the detection space and transmits this information to the operator. The data is collected by sensors that are designed to capture some form of energy (see sec. 3.4.2) that contains information about the detection space or about objects in the detection space. Because the sensors and objects in the detection space are not in physical contact, the energy that is collected must be some type of radiating or propagating energy, and this energy must contain information on objects in the detection space. This collected (detected) energy is then used by the CWCIDS to provide an indication, an image, etc., to the operator regarding the objects in the detection space of the CWCIDS.

5.1 Sources of the Detected Energy

The energy detected by the CWCIDS is either emitted, transmitted, or reflected by objects in the detection space. If the CWCIDS uses either reflected or transmitted energy to provide information on the detection space, then the detection space must be illuminated. This illumination may be provided by the environment (for passive illumination, see sec. 5.1.1) or the CWCIDS (for active illumination, see sec. 5.1.3). The energy that illuminates objects in the detection space is called the incident energy. The CWCIDS detects only that part of the incident energy that is reflected by or transmitted through objects within the detection space. It is this reflected or transmitted energy that carries information on the objects in the detection space and that can be used to form an image or provide an indication. The CWCIDS may also use energy that was emitted by the objects in the detection space to gather information on the objects in the detection space; this situation is described in section 5.1.2.

5.1.1 Passive Illumination

In passive illumination, the CWCIDS uses naturally occurring radiation and/or ambient anthropogenic sources of radiation to obtain information about objects in the detection space. The naturally occurring sources of radiation (or energy) can be found inside or outside of the detection space. The sun, for example, is a natural source of energy that is outside of the detection space. Other natural sources of energy that can illuminate the detection space are other "hot" objects (black-body sources, see sec. 5.1.2) located within or outside of the detection space. Ambient anthropogenic sources of energy are such things as radios, telecommunication devices, vehicles, etc., and these sources provide background energy (or noise) that can be used to illuminate the detection space of a CWCIDS. This type of anthropogenic radiation will be more prevalent in densely populated areas than in sparsely populated rural areas.

The energy that illuminates the detection space is reflected, absorbed, and transmitted by objects within the detection space. Although the CWCIDS can use either the reflected or transmitted energy to gather information on objects in the detection space, most CWCIDSs use the reflected energy. Daytime photography is a good example of an imaging system that uses passive illumination. For photography, the natural energy source is the sun and the image of the detection space is obtained from the reflected light.

The quality of the information acquired from passive-illumination CWCIDS is affected by the absorption of energy by innocuous items inside or outside of the detection space. A simple example of the effect of absorption is a piece of cloth in front of a camera lens. In this example, the absorption of light by the cloth destroys the image. The effects of absorption of energy by a material is described in section 5.4.1.

5.1.2 Black-Body Radiation

The passive CWCIDS may also use the naturally occurring radiation emitted by a "hot" object in the detection space to obtain information about that hot object. "Hot" is relative and, in this case, it means anything that does not have a temperature of absolute zero (-273 • C or, equivalently, -459 • F). The emission of radiation from a hot object is usually referred to as black-body radiation and the hot object as a black-body radiator. The black-body radiator emits energy over a range of wavelengths and the peak emission of a black-body radiator is dependent on the temperature of the body. The total amount of power emitted from a body at a given temperature is dependent on the mass of the body and the material that comprises the object. Most objects are not ideal black-body radiators because of their material composition.

The energy emitted by an ideal black-body radiator is well known. For example, the curve in figure 4 shows the black-body emittance (given in units of power per area, such as Watts per square meter) curve for a body at 37 • C (98.6 • F), the average temperature of a human body. The curve shows the relative emittance for a given object at different wavelengths. (A discussion of wavelengths is given in sec. 5.4.) We can see from the figure that, for the typical temperature of a human body, the human emittance peaks at a wavelength of approximately 10 μm (1 000 000 μm is equal to 1 m). The reason many thermal imaging systems are designed to have a peak detection sensitivity around 10 μm is so that people can be more readily imaged. Thermal imaging is the term frequently used to describe imaging based on black-body radiation.

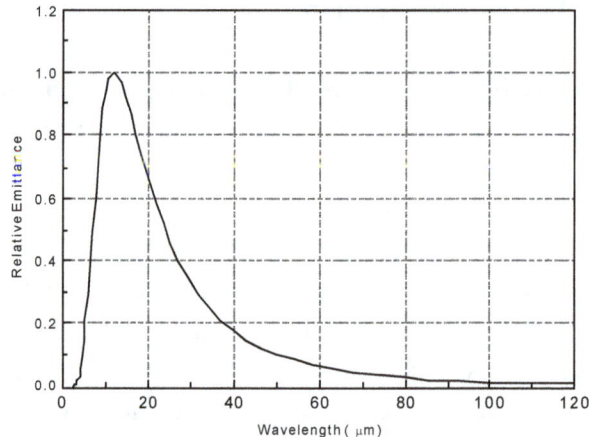

Figure 4. Black-body emittance curve for a body at 37 • C

16

The information obtained by a CWCIDS using thermal detection can be affected by the absorption of black-body radiation by innocuous items (such as clothing, paper, etc.) located inside the detection space and between the object and the detector or source. This absorption masks the emission of target items. Also, the target items may reflect energy emitted by hotter objects located inside or outside the detection space, and this reflected energy will affect the quality of the information obtained by a thermal-imaging CWCIDS.

5.1.3 Active Illumination

In active illumination, the CWCIDS supplies the energy that is used to illuminate the detection space and, therefore, the active-illumination CWCIDS must contain a subsystem for generating and emitting energy. The illuminating (or incident) energy is reflected from, absorbed by, and transmitted through objects in the detection space. The reflected energy is typically used to form the image or provide an indication (see fig. 5) of objects in the detection space, but the transmitted energy could also be used. The amount of energy that is reflected from objects in the detection space depends on the reflectivity and absorptivity of all the objects in the detection space (see secs. 5.4.2 and 5.4.1). The reflected energy collected for any target object located in the detection space is affected not only by the properties of that target object but also by the properties of other objects located inside the detection space and to some extent by objects located outside the detection space. The reflected energy for a target object is affected by the existence of the other objects because these other objects can mask the energy reflected by the target object. Masking can be accomplished by absorbing the energy reflected by the target object (as mentioned in sec. 5.1.2) and by reflecting away from the CWCIDS detector the energy reflected by the target objected. Innocuous objects in the detection zone may also reflect significant energy to the CWCIDS detector. Masking of the target object by reflection (see sec. 5.4.2) may also be accomplished by objects outside of the detection space. An example of active illumination in an imaging application is flash photography. In flash photography, the backdrop material must not be highly reflecting because reflections from the backdrop may dominate the image.

The information collected by an active-illuminating CWCIDS on a target object is affected by the absorption, reflectivity, and transmissivity of innocuous items within and outside of the detection space and by other sources of energy (including black-body radiators). The effect of these other sources of energy on the CWCIDS is dependent on the wavelength(s) of their emitted energy compared to the wavelength(s) of energy emitted by the source and on the sensitivity of the detector to wavelengths different from

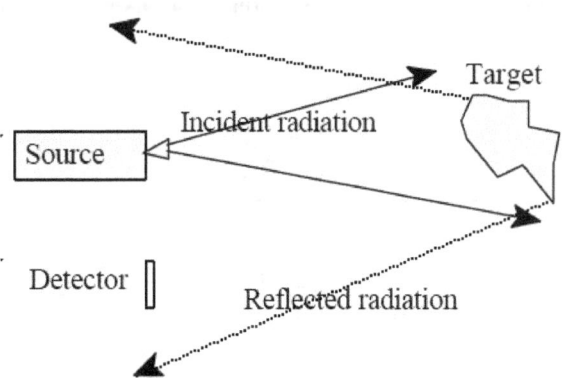

Figure 5. Active imaging system and target

17

that of the source signal.

5.2 Forms of Detected Energy

The CWCIDS requires input of some form of energy, such as light, microwave, or acoustic energy, to provide an image or an indication. There are two very general types of energy that can be used by a CWCIDS to probe or interrogate a detection space: acoustic and electromagnetic energy. This section will describe the forms of energy that are used in CWCIDSs, the sources of this energy, and other aspects of radiation that are important to understand the CWCIDS operation.

5.2.1 Acoustic Energy

Acoustic energy is the energy associated with pressure waves and for CWCIDS applications, the waves will be propagating in air. Our ears are sensitive to acoustic energy. Human hearing primarily provides an indication of the magnitude of the sound source with minimal information on the location of the sound source. Some animals, however, can use their hearing to accurately locate the position of a sound source. The different tones we hear are caused by different wavelengths (see sec. 5.4) of the acoustic energy. The lower the pitch, the longer the wavelength. Ultrasonic (frequencies exceeding the upper limit of human detection) energy is used in medicine for generating images within the body, such as of a fetus in the uterus. Sonar is another example of acoustic energy that is used for detection and location of objects. With sonar, however, the medium of wave propagation is water. Acoustic waves propagate better in dense media (solids and liquids) than in sparse media (gasses). An acoustic wave will not propagate in a vacuum (volume without any matter), such as outer space.

5.2.2 Electromagnetic Energy

Electromagnetic energy is the energy associated with electromagnetic waves, and electric and magnetic fields. Sunlight, x-rays, infrared, microwaves, and radio waves are all electromagnetic waves. The only difference between these different types of electromagnetic waves is their wavelength (see fig. 6). The

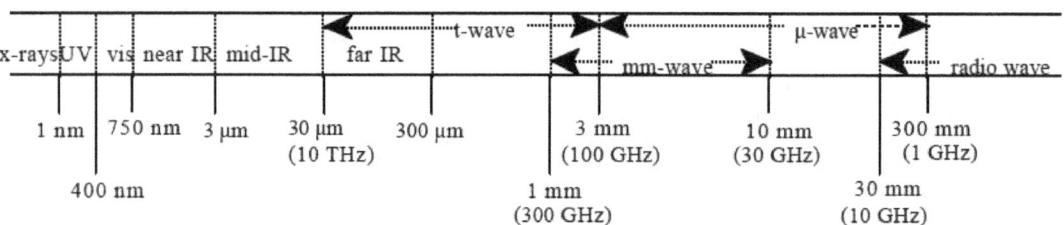

Figure 6. Electromagnetic spectrum

18

wavelength (given in meters) of an electromagnetic wave is related to its frequency of oscillation (given in cycles per second or Hz). There is also energy associated with magnetic and electric fields. The energy associated with static magnetic fields can be readily experienced if one tries to force the north (or south) poles of two magnets together; magnetic fields are discussed in section 5.2.3. See reference 1 (sec. 9) or a similar text for an introduction to electromagnetic waves.

5.2.2.1 Magnetic Field

Magnetic field energy is that associated with magnetic fields (see ref. 2 listed in sec. 9 or similar text), including those produced by artificial means and that produced by the earth's magnetic field. Stationary magnetic fields are also a type of energy, but they are considered separately in this section because the previous section dealt with radiative electromagnetic fields. The stationary magnetic fields that are produced by artificial means or by the earth do not propagate as electromagnetic waves: however, they may have electric fields associated with them. This association of an electric field with the magnetic field is important in the detection of metal objects as will be described in section 5.5.

5.3 Sources of Electromagnetic Radiation

Electromagnetic (EM) radiation is made of waves that vary in amplitude, similar to how the ac voltage in our homes varies (see fig. 7). The variation of the wave shown in figure 7 is said to be sinusoidal. There are two very general sources of electromagnetic radiation: coherent and incoherent (sec. 5.3.1).

5.3.1 Coherent vs. Incoherent

Coherency describes how well two waves stay in step as they travel away from the energy source that generated them. More precisely, the separation between a specific point on one wave

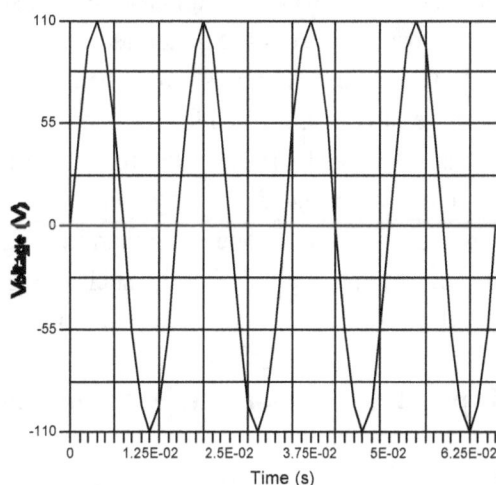

Figure 7. Sinusoidally-varying ac voltage

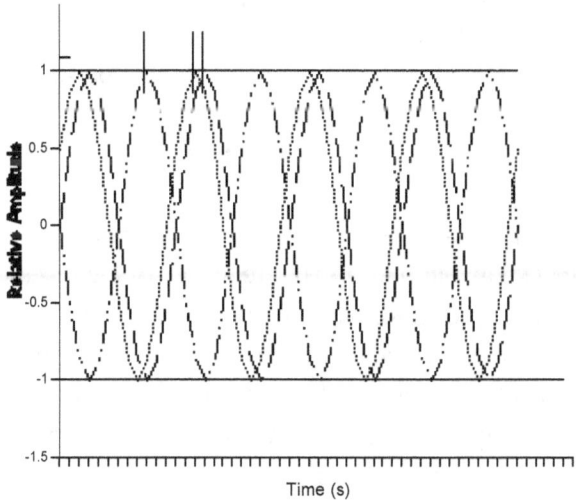

Figure 8. Three sinusoidal waves that are not in phase (in step); the vertical lines help show the degree to which the three waves are out of step and the horizontal lines define the envelope of the waves

19

and a specific point on the other wave stays the same as the waves travel together. As an example, consider the three waves shown in figure 8. The three waves in figure 8 are not aligned with each other and the vertical lines that are located at the crests of the waves can be used to measure the misalignment of the waves. This measure is also called the phase relationship of the waves. Coherent waves maintain their phase relationship as they travel away from the source. Incoherent waves, on the other hand, do not have any fixed phase relationship. That is, the distance between crests of waves varies as soon as the waves are generated. There are various degrees of coherency, and this degree is based on how far the waves must travel before the phase relationship changes. A nonelectromagnetic-wave example of coherency is a line of people marching side-by-side. Regardless of what foot the marchers start with, as long as all the marchers in the line keep the same pace and the same stride as they march, the marchers are moving coherently. Lasers are sources of highly coherent radiation. Radars are also sources of coherent radiation. Light bulbs and the sun are sources of incoherent radiation. In general, any "hot" body, such as the sun, a light bulb, and a person, is a black-body radiator and is a source of incoherent radiation.

5.3.2 Types of Sources for Active Illumination

The active-illumination CWCIDS uses a source of energy to illuminate the detection space. These sources of energy are typed or classified, for the purposes of this Guide, based on the time characteristics of the emitted (or output) power. This emitted power may have a variety of different time characteristics and these characteristics are used by the CWCIDS designers to improve signal quality. One type of source is called a continuous-wave (cw) source (see sec. 5.3.2.1). Continuous-wave sources are used in laser pointers, laser scanners in supermarkets, etc. Continuous-wave sources may be modulated in many ways, including frequency modulation and amplitude modulation. The other generic type of source is the pulse source; pulse sources emit pulses of energy (see sec. 5.3.2.2).

5.3.2.1 Continuous Wave Sources

A continuous-wave (cw) source emits an unbroken repeating wave of electromagnetic energy (similar to that shown in fig. 7). The frequency of the repeats of the electromagnetic wave of a cw signal is often called the information carrying (or carrier) frequency. The straight horizontal lines in figure 8 indicate the upper and lower bounds (the envelope) of the cw amplitude. Continuous-wave sources can also be modulated; that is, the cw energy can be forced to vary in some way. The advantage of modulating a cw source is that it is often much easier and more effective to sense and analyze the modulated signal than the un-modulated signal. Examples of modulation are amplitude modulation (AM) and frequency modulation (FM). Modulation is accomplished using electronic circuits. In amplitude modulation, the envelope of the cw signal varies. The modulation envelope of an amplitude modulated signal is sinusoidal, and the repeat frequency of the envelope sinusoid is much lower than the carrier frequency. In frequency modulation, the carrier frequency is varied slightly. Most modulation schemes were developed for communication and broadcast applications. The output of a cw source is typically expressed as an average power with units of watts.

5.3.2.2 Pulse Sources

A pulse source emits pulses of electromagnetic energy (see fig. 9). The energy emitted by a pulse source is spread over many frequencies whereas the energy emitted by a cw source is primarily at one frequency, the carrier frequency. Moreover, pulse sources typically produce significantly more peak power than cw sources produce average power. The advantage of high peak power for an active CWCIDS is that greater power means improved system performance, and this results in superior image clarity and/or faster imaging rates. The output power of a pulse source is typically expressed as an energy with units of Joules per pulse or as a peak power with units of watts.

5.3.2.3 The Effect of Source Power on Signal Quality

The reason higher source powers typically produce better images is a signal to noise issue. If the dominant source of noise is not the source, the increased signal amplitude relative to the noise will improve image quality. Remember, the reflected power provides information on objects in the detection space. With higher source power, more power will be reflected by the objects in the detection space and subsequently be collected by the CWCIDS detector. In addition to collecting the reflected power, the detectors also respond to the background power. The background power is noise and is very undesirable. Noise degrades the quality of the collected information and the effects of noise on the signal must be reduced. Noise can come from a variety of sources, such as non-target-item black-bodies, other electronics, etc. In addition to these noise sources, unwanted reflections can also degrade the quality of the signal for CWCIDSs using active illumination. Unwanted reflections come from the incident energy that has reflected from objects outside of the detection space and from multipath reflections within the detection space that are collected by the CWCIDS. Multipath reflections (much like bullet ricochets) come from energy that was reflected multiple times from objects in the detection space as shown in figure 10. In figure 10, the line

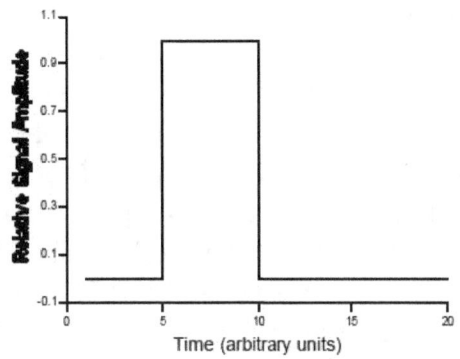

Figure 9. Rectangular envelope for pulse modulation

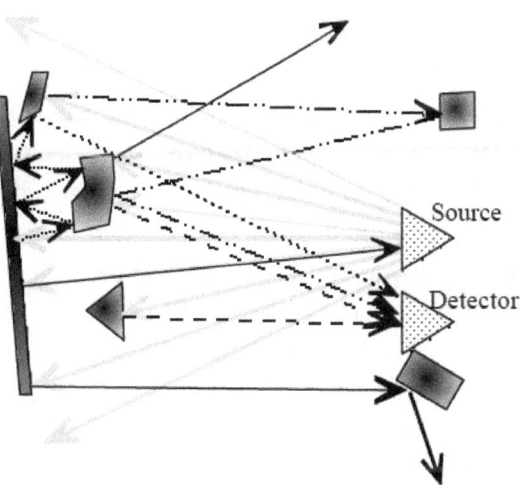

Figure 10. Signal paths in the detection space (see sec. 5.3.2.3 for an explanation of the lines)

21

representation is as follows: heavy solid lines represent the incident energy, the light solid lines indicate the reflected energy that was not collected by the detector, the dashed lines represent the energy that was reflected from objects in the detection space and collected after one reflection, the dotted lines represent the energy collected after many reflections between objects inside the detection space, and the dashed-dotted lines represent the energy collected after multiple reflections between objects inside and outside the detection space.

A term that is frequently used to describe the quality of a detector is the detector's signal-to-noise ratio (SNR). The SNR is the ratio of the power of a noise-free signal to the power of the noise. The larger the SNR, the better will be the signal. Moreover, the greater the SNR, the faster the information can be gathered by the CWCIDS; speed is very important for imaging, tracking, and surveillance. Higher SNRs lead to faster imaging speed because less signal averaging is required to achieve a given image quality. Higher incident powers typically lead to higher SNRs.

5.3.4 Magnetic Field Sources

The earth is a source of magnetic fields. Magnetic fields can also be generated by passing an electrical current through a wire (see fig. 11). The magnetic field produced from the wire is depicted in figure 11. Wrapping the wire into a coil results in the addition of the magnetic fields produced by each turn of the

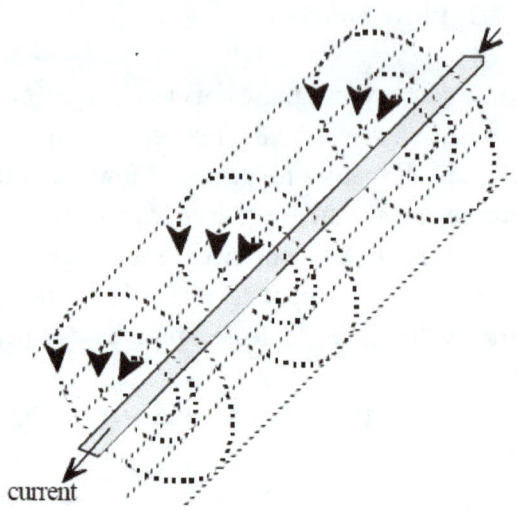

Figure 11. The magnetic field lines wrap around a current carrying wire

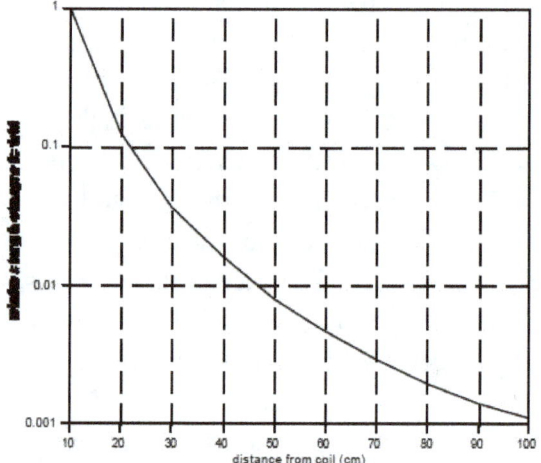

Figure 12. The intensity of the magnetic field at various distances from the source coil

coil. The circles that wrap around the wire represent the magnetic field intensity; the farther away these circles are from the wire, the lower is the intensity of the magnetic field. The circuit and coil for generating the magnetic field is called the source. Figure 12 shows how the intensity of the magnetic field drops off as one moves away from the source coil. As can be seen in figure 12, the field strength drops off very quickly.

5.4 Electromagnetic Wave Interactions

22

The electromagnetic wave interactions with an object are affected by the length of the wave and the wavelength dependent properties of the object. The wavelength is the distance between two identical points on a continuous wave (see figs. 7 and 8), such as distance between adjacent crests. As mentioned earlier, the difference between x-rays and infrared is their wavelength. The wavelength of the energy has several effects on the performance of a CWCIDS, and these effects are the result of the wavelength-dependent absorption (sec. 5.4.1) by, the wavelength-dependent reflection (see sec. 5.4.2) from, and the wavelength-dependent transmission (see sec. 5.4.3) through objects in the detection space, and of the interference (sec. 5.4.4) caused by objects in the detection space. Recall, all of the energy incident on the detection space is either reflected, transmitted, and/or absorbed. The transmission through, absorption in, and reflection from objects in the detection space is dependent on the geometries of the objects and their material composition. Whether or not the material-related or geometry-related effects are helpful or deleterious is dependent on whether the objects being searched (the target items) are producing these effects or being masked by these effects. See references 3, 4, and 5 listed in section 9 or similar texts for more information on the interaction of electromagnetic waves with matter.

5.4.1 Absorption

Absorption of energy affects all CWCIDSs. Whether absorption is useful or not depends on whether the absorption adds to the information about target objects (weapons and contraband) in the detection space or masks information about target objects in the detection space. Both target items and innocuous items (such as clothing) absorb energy. In general, information is added if the target items absorb energy whereas information is lost if the innocuous items absorb energy. A situation where absorption would not be good is if an explosive material or weapon is not detected because it was enclosed in an energy absorbing box. In many situations, the human body is a very effective absorbing object.

5.4.1.1 Causes of Absorption

The absorption of acoustic or electromagnetic energy by an object is dependent on several properties of the object and on the wavelength of the radiation. There are different mechanisms for absorption depending on the type and wavelength of the energy. For example, absorption of visible light is attributed to the electrons in the atoms that comprise an object, specifically the valence or outer electrons. X-ray absorption is also caused by electrons in atoms, but this time it is by the core or inner electrons. For microwave radiation, the absorption is attributed to the atoms within a molecule. Microwave absorption by a molecule causes the atoms of the molecule to vibrate and these vibrations generate heat. This is how a microwave oven cooks food. Acoustic energy can also be absorbed. Acoustic absorption is dependent on the density and structural rigidity of the object.

Different materials have different electronic and atomic environments and, therefore, have different absorptivities. For pure materials, the wavelength-dependent absorption of energy can be used to uniquely identify the material.

5.4.2 Reflection

Reflection of energy from an object is dependent on the material composition of the object (see sec. 5.4.2.1), the geometry and size of the object (see sec. 5.4.2.4), the size of features on the object (see sec. 5.4.2.4), and the wavelength of the energy. Size-related effects can be described, in general, as diffraction (see sec. 5.4.2.4) effects. Reflection will also be dependent on the orientation of the object with respect to the incident energy (see sec. 5.4.2.2) and the surface roughness of the object (see sec. 5.4.2.3). The difference between reflectivities and absorptivities of materials is what makes photographs possible.

Reflectivity is the basis on which most active-illumination and passive-illumination CWCIDSs rely to obtain information on the detection space. Nevertheless, as mentioned in section 5.3.2.3, multipath reflections within the detection space and reflections from objects outside of the detection space are undesirable because they affect CWCIDS performance by decreasing the SNR. In addition, wavelength-dependent reflection affects the spatial resolution (image sharpness) of imaging-type CWCIDSs and the detection ability of detection-type CWCIDSs. Wavelength-dependent reflection and absorption is encountered daily and is how we perceive color.

5.4.2.1 Materials

The electromagnetic-wave reflectivity of materials is dependent on the electronic and optical properties and the microscopic structure of the material. Electromagnetic material properties that can affect signal quality are electrical conductivity, magnetic permeability, and dielectric permittivity (or dielectric constant). Acoustic reflectivity is dependent on the hardness of the material and the structure of the object. Acoustic properties that can affect signal quality are material density, hardness, and stiffness.

5.4.2.2 Orientation

The intensity of the energy reflected by an object is dependent on the orientation of the surface of the object with respect to the incident radiation. A commonly encountered example of orientation-dependent reflectivity is the reflection of light from a glass surface. If a glass plate is oriented such that the angle between the surface of the plate and the object is small, the glass will exhibit a very high reflectivity (like a mirror) and the object can easily be seen in the reflection from the glass surface. Looking directly at the glass plate, on the other hand, only gives a faint image of your face. Typically, the reflectivity of the glass plate can vary between 5 % and 95 % depending on the viewing angle. Orientation effects are dependent on the wavelength of energy and the material composition of the reflecting object.

5.4.2.3 Surface Roughness

The roughness of a surface, relative to the wavelength of incident energy, affects the amount of energy that is reflected in a particular direction by an object. The rougher the surface, the poorer the directional reflectivity of the surface. The effect of surface roughness can be described using figure 13. As shown in the figure, the rough surface acts as if it is comprised of many miniature mirrors and each mini-mirror reflects the incident energy in a different direction. If the wavelength of the energy is large compared to the size of the mini-mirrors, the mini-mirrors do not affect the reflectivity of the surface. This type of reflection where the incident energy is scattered is called diffuse reflection. The smooth surface, on the other hand (see the bottom surface of fig. 13),

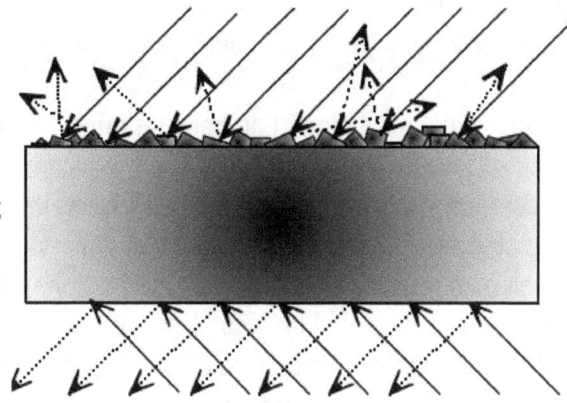

Figure 13. The effect of surface roughness on reflectivity

reflects the incident radiation in only one direction. This type of reflection is called specular reflection. A smooth surface, in the context of reflectivity, is one in which the surface roughness is much less than a wavelength. A common example that illustrates the effect of surface roughness on the reflectivity of an object is a sanded or polished surface. The polished surface has a much higher reflectivity than a sanded surface.

5.4.2.4 Diffraction

Diffraction occurs when the dimensions of an object or its features are about a wavelength or less in length and is a result of interference (see sec. 5.4.4). Diffraction also occurs at the edges of objects. The best way to understand diffraction is to consider figure 14. There are two objects that are being illuminated by waves, a pin and a plate. The pin is very small and the plate is very large compared to the wavelength of the incident energy. Illumination of the pin results in small circular waves that are reflected outward and away from the pin in almost all directions: this is diffraction. Illumination of the plate, on the other hand, results in a plane wave that is reflected back toward the source. Note,

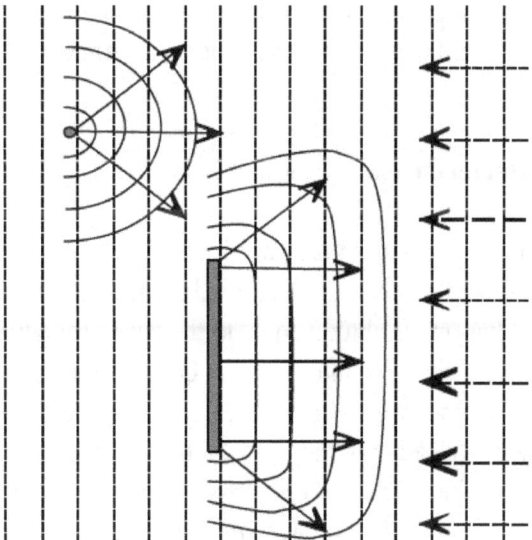

Figure 14. Sketch showing diffraction from an object where the dashed vertical lines indicate the incident waves, the solid lines indicate the reflected waves, and the arrows indicate direction of wave propagation

however, that the edges of the plate also diffract the incident waves. Diffraction will also occur for features on a large object where the features are smaller than a wavelength of the incident energy.

The lateral spatial resolution of an image is affected by diffraction because, as shown in figure 14, if the reflecting surface is not large relative to a wavelength, then a circular wavefront propagates from the object and forms a blurry spot image. As long as the object is much smaller than a wavelength, many different objects will generate the same circular wavefront and the same blurry spot. Consequently, if the wavelength is much longer than the dimensions of the object to be imaged, no decipherable image or only a blurry image will be seen. Thus, no object will be detected. As the wavelength is decreased, a distorted image may start to appear. As the wavelength is decreased even further, the image starts to attain greater and greater spatial resolution because now a plane wave is reflected from the object and this plane wave carries information on the extent of that surface. A common example of the effect of diffraction on imaging is the light microscope. Light microscopes are used to see microscopic objects down to about the size of a cell. Smaller objects, such as the insides of the cell or most viruses require an electron microscope to be seen.

5.4.3 Transmission

Transmission of energy affects all CWCIDSs. Transmissivity describes the properties of a material that allows energy to pass through an object made of that material. Transmission, reflection, and absorption are related; the energy that is neither reflected or absorbed is transmitted. For acoustic energy, most liquids and hard solids are good acoustic transmitters. Glass is a good transmitter of visible light and infrared. If the target object has a high transmittance to the incident radiation, the object will be difficult to find.

5.4.4 Interference

Interference is a result of the wave nature (see fig. 7) of the radiated energy and the alignment of waves (see fig. 8). If two waves are aligned so that their crests overlap, the result is the appearance of a single wave that has an amplitude equal to the sum of the two overlapping waves. That is, we see one large wave instead of two smaller waves. On the other hand, if the crests of one wave are aligned with the valleys of another wave, the result is a wave with no amplitude; that is, we see no waves. To emphasize: we see only the result of the addition of the two waves (or, if there are many waves, of all the waves). This observed change in the wave amplitude that is caused by the interaction between two or more waves is called interference. Interference can be constructive, destructive, or somewhere in between depending on how well aligned are the crests of the waves. The energy collected by a detector is dependent on the interference between reflected waves that are incident on the detector. The more destructive the interference is between waves incident on the detector, the less is the power collected by the detector. In the extreme case of destructive interference at the detector (crests of one wave are aligned with valleys of another wave), no signal is observed. In a CWCIDS, interference can be caused by objects inside or outside the detection space.

5.5 Magnetic Field Interactions

The magnetic field produced by a source may interact with a nearby object. Whether an interaction occurs and the type and strength of this interaction depends on the type of material that the object is made of (see sec. 5.5.1.1), the size (sec. 5.5.1.2) and shape (sec. 5.5.1.2) of the object, the orientation of the object in the magnetic field (sec. 5.5.1.2), and the speed of the object through the magnetic field.

The earth's magnetic field may interact with a moving object. There are two requirements to detect the interaction of the earth's magnetic field with an object. One requirement is that the object has to be moving perpendicular to the earth's magnetic field lines. The second requirement is that the object must be comprised of a material that has a relative permeability not equal to one. The larger the relative permeability, the easier it is to detect a body.

For an object to interact with the magnetic field, either the magnetic field must be time-varying, as is the case for active magnetic-field-based CWCIDS, or the object has to be moving with respect to the stationary magnetic field, as is the case for passive magnetic-field-based CWCIDS.

5.5.1 Object Properties that Affect Detection

There are a variety of object properties that can affect the detectability of the object. Although many of these properties are similar to those that affect detection for an electromagnetic-wave-based CWCIDS, the interaction mechanism is different. For example, the conductivity of a metal object will affect the reflectivity of electromagnetic waves whereas in a magnetic-field-based CWCIDS, the conductivity will affect the generation of eddy currents (see sec. 5.5.1.1). See reference 6 listed in section 9 for more information on the operation of hand-held and walk-through metal detectors.

5.5.1.1 Materials

Each material has a unique set of electromagnetic properties. Therefore, a group of objects that are identical (shape, size, etc.) except for their material composition will each have a unique signal. That is, the interaction between the object and the source magnetic field will be different for each object. Two characteristics of the material that will determine the strength of the interaction are the electrical conductivity and the magnetic permeability of that material. The electrical conductivity and magnetic permeability of an object allow two different paths for interactions with the source magnetic field. Although the source magnetic field may induce a temporary magnetization in the object, which may be detected, the primary source of interaction is the induction of an electrical current, which is detected.

The electrical conductivity describes the ease at which electrical charge can move (or flow) in a material. A material that allows electrical charge to flow is called a conductor. For metals, the electrical charge is carried by electrons. In certain solutions, like salt water, the electrical charge is carried by ions. To get an idea of the variation in the electrical conductivity of different materials, see

27

table 1. The units of conductivity are Siemens per meter (S/m). The electrical conductivity of human tissue is about equal to that of sea water (see table 1).

The flow of electrical charge in a conductor is analogous to water flow in a pipe: the higher the conductance of a pipe, the easier it is for water to flow in the pipe. It does require, however, a force to make the water flow. Similarly, for an electrical charge to flow in a conductor requires an external force.

Table 1. Electrical conductivity of some materials (see ref. 1 listed in sec. 9)

Material	Conductivity (S/m)
copper	57,000,000
aluminum	35,000,000
brass	11,000,000
lead	5,000,000
stainless steel	2,000,000
cast iron	1,000,000
graphite	100,000
sea water	4
distilled water	• 0.0001
Bakelite	• 0.000000001
glass	• 0.000000000001
diamond	• 0.0000000000001
air	0.

The magnetic field produced by the source may cause (or induce) a current to flow in a nearby conductive object; this induced current is called an eddy current. The magnitude of the induced current is dependent on the object's electrical conductivity (and other properties). However, not all magnetic fields can induce an eddy current; the magnetic field must be changing with time (see fig. 7). The eddy currents induced in an object by the external magnetic field can themselves induce magnetic fields in other objects. The magnitude of the eddy current that is induced in the object by the source (or primary) magnetic field is dependent on the electrical conductivity of the object. A very poor conductor, such as graphite, will support only a very small eddy current. On the other hand, a very good conductor, such as gold, silver, aluminum, or copper, can support a much larger eddy current.

The magnetic permeability also affects the magnitude of the induced eddy current. The effect of the permeability, in this case, as compared to magnetizing the object, is to alter the magnitude of the associated electric field inside the object. Larger permeability values (see table 2) mean larger associated electric fields and this means larger eddy currents.

The reference for relative permeability is a vacuum because a vacuum has no particles that can interact with the magnetic field: the relative permeability of a vacuum is 1. Air is typically given a relative permeability of 1 because there are so few particles (molecules, atoms, etc.) that can interact with the magnetic field. Relative permeability values can be slightly less than 1 (for what is called diamagnetic materials), slightly more than 1 (for paramagnetic materials), and much greater than 1 (for ferromagnetic materials). For this application, if a material behaves like air in terms of its permeability, then a magnetic field will not measurably magnetize the material. Table 2 lists some materials and their relative permeability values. When the relative permeability of a material is much larger than 1, then the material will noticeably affect the source magnetic field.

Common magnetic materials are listed in table 2. Magnetism is caused by the electrons in an atom. There are many different ways that the electrons may interact with each other in a material, and these interactions are the basis for magnetic-based classification of materials (see far right column in table 2). Ferromagnetic materials possess microscopic domains that allow objects made from these materials to easily interact with an externally-applied magnetic field, like those magnetic fields produced by hand-held (HH) and walk-through (WT) metal detectors. The other types of magnetic materials (see table 2) do not easily interact with an applied magnetic field.

Table 2. Relative permeability and magnetic classification of some materials (see ref. 1 listed in sec. 9)

Material	Relative Permeability	Classification
supermalloy	1,000,000	ferromagnetic
purified iron	200,000	ferromagnetic
iron (0.2% impurities)	5000	ferromagnetic
mild steel (0.2 % carbon)	2000	ferromagnetic
nickel	600	ferromagnetic
cobalt	250	ferromagnetic
aluminum	1.00002	paramagnetic
air	1.0000004	paramagnetic
vacuum	1.	nonmagnetic
water	0.999991	diamagnetic
copper	0.999991	diamagnetic
lead	0.999983	diamagnetic
silver	0.99983	diamagnetic

5.5.1.2 Other Object Properties

Each object, due to its mass alone, will have a unique signal. For example, a sugar-cube-sized or brick-sized piece of aluminum will not give the same signal. The brick-sized object will give a larger signal. However, two objects with the same mass and with the same material composition may cause different levels of response by a HH or WT unit.

Orientation of the object in the primary magnetic field has an effect on HH and WT detection performance because the source (primary) magnetic field is directional. The importance of object orientation in relation to the direction of the magnetic field is that, to generate an eddy current, the magnetic field or a component of the magnetic field has to be perpendicular to a surface of the object. This is discussed in more detail in reference 6 listed in section 9.

Other object properties also affect object detection, such as, object shape, multiple objects in the detection space, frequency of the time-varying magnetic field, etc. These topics are described in reference 6.

6. SAFETY AND RADIATION EXPOSURE

A very important issue to the LEC community is human exposure to the energy emitted by active-illumination CWCIDSs and the potential risk of that radiation to human health. Passive-illumination CWCIDSs and black-body-based CWCIDSs do not intentionally emit energy and, therefore, do not pose any additional health risks compared to other electronic devices. The energies and powers emitted by active-illumination CWCIDSs are typically much below that considered by the U.S. Food and Drug Administration (USFDA) to be a threat to the health of an average person. However, the potential health threat to people using personal medical electronic devices, such as cardiac pacemakers, cardiac defibrillators, etc., may be different. It is recommended, therefore, that if an agency has a safety question or concern regarding a CWCIDS, that agency should contact their local consumer information office of the USFDA. If the agency has difficulty in locating a local consumer information office, they should contact the FDA at their internet address: http://www.fda.gov.

7. THE TECHNOLOGIES

The different CWCIDSs are described in this section and are arranged first by the phenomena (magnetic field, electromagnetic wave, acoustic wave, see sec. 5.2) used for detection, then whether the CWCIDS uses active or passive illumination, and lastly by the proximity of use. As described in section 5.1.3, active-illumination CWCIDSs are systems that generate and emit some sort of energy that is used to illuminate the detection space. A passive-illumination CWCIDS, on the other hand, does not intentionally generate or emit energy. A passive-illumination system uses the natural background energy for illumination of the detection space. Table 3 provides a brief summary of the different technologies described in this Guide. References to the different technologies are provided for those interested in more detailed information. However, not all the systems described have published articles on which to base a reference.

Requirements for a detector/imager will vary with the specific application of the LEC agency. The LEC agency must consider the following parameters when selecting a CWCIDS: material composition of the target objects, size of the target objects, expected location of the target objects (such as on the surface of a body, in a body cavity, buried in the ground, etc.), detection versus imaging, experience and training of the officer or operator, speed of operation, and information quality (clarity of images for an imaging system and false alarm rate for a detection system). Additional concerns are deployment of the CWCIDS, purchase costs, maintenance costs, privacy issues, and utility (power, cooling, etc.) requirements.

When reviewing literature describing the ability of these CWCIDSs to find concealed weapons, whether that literature is sales brochures or technical articles, the reader should carefully examine the data that is presented. In many cases, the information, although not incorrect, may not be complete and may be misleading. If there is difficulty in understanding the information provided by a manufacturer, whether that information is a published technical article or an advertisement brochure, contact the Office of Law Enforcement Standards or the National Institute of Justice to help clarify that information.

7.1 Acoustic-Based Hard Object Detector

Presently, there exists one fully developed weapon detector based on acoustic wave phenomena. This device is a hand-held, light-weight unit that can be used to find weapons hidden on an individual between 1 m and 5 m away. Consequently, these acoustic devices can be used to find objects located and/or concealed on a person a few meters from the LEC officer. The acoustic detector presently being tested is a light-weight, battery-operated, low-cost (less than $200 each), easy-to-use unit. To facilitate directing the acoustic beam onto a target location, the unit contains a focused light beam that is aligned with the emitted acoustic beam. See reference 8 listed in section 9 for more details.

Table 3. A tabulation of the different technologies described in this guide

DESCRIPTION	SECTION	ENERGY	ILLUMINATION	PROXIMITY	PORTABILITY
hard object detector	7.1	acoustic	active	far	portable
WT metal object detector	7.2	magnetic	active	near	transportable
HH metal object detector	7.3	magnetic	active	near	portable
imaging portal	7.4	magnetic	active	near	transportable
body cavity imager	7.5	magnetic	active	near	fixed-site
ferromagnetic metal detector	7.6	magnetic	passive	near	transportable
metal object locator	7.7	magnetic	passive	far	transportable
μwave holographic imager	7.8	EM wave	active	near	transportable
μwave dielectrometer imager	7.9	EM wave	active	near	transportable
x-ray imager	7.10	EM wave	active	near	transportable
μwave radar imager	7.11	EM wave	active	far	transportable
pulse radar/ swept frequency detector	7.12	EM wave	active	far	transportable
mm-wave/THz-wave imager	7.13	EM wave	active	far	transportable
mm-wave radar detector	7.14	EM wave	active	far	hand-held
EM pulse detector	7.15	EM wave	active	far	transportable
mm-wave imager	7.16	EM wave	passive	far	transportable
IR imager	7.17	EM wave	passive	far	transportable
mm-wave/IR imager	7.18	EM wave	passive	far	transportable

34

7.1.1 Theory of Operation

The detection of a weapon/contraband item is dependent on the acoustic reflectivity of the materials that make up the object, and the shape and orientation of the object. Basically, hard objects will provide a high acoustic reflectivity and soft objects a small acoustic reflectivity. Consequently, this technology can be used to find plastic weapons as well as metal weapons. The flat surfaces that are perpendicular to the incident acoustic wave will provide the largest detectable return signal. The important detection parameters for this technology are size of the target object, diameter of the detector antenna, wavelength of the emitted acoustic power, and the emitted power. The antenna size and wavelength affect the size of the smallest object that can be detected; to a limit, the larger the antenna and the shorter the wavelength, the smaller an object can be and still be detected (see sec. 5.4). The primary limitation on the antenna size is the requirement that the detector be hand-held and easily carried by LEC officers. Transmission of the acoustic power is also a concern. As was stated in section 5.2.1, acoustic power will not travel in a vacuum; acoustic energy is attenuated less as it travels in dense medium, such as solids and liquids, and is attenuated more as it propagates in gases, such as air. The humidity in air reduces the attenuation of an acoustic wave. Therefore, if the object size is inferred from the signal amplitude, then the effects of humidity must be accommodated; this accommodation is done in the present acoustic detector. The attenuation (power loss) of the acoustic power is also very strongly frequency dependent; attenuation is greater for higher frequencies. Therefore, there is a trade-off in the required spatial resolution and the amount of attenuation that can be allowed before detection of a target item is affected. The power of the emitted acoustic energy is limited by the ability to generate the energy and safety. Consequently, the acoustic power cannot be increased arbitrarily to compensate for losses in the air.

7.1.2 Considerations for Use

The acoustic-based detector is sensitive to hard objects in general and, therefore, its present design cannot differentiate between weapons and contraband items, and innocuous hard objects. In fact, for the wavelengths of the acoustic energy used by these devices, leather also causes a large acoustic reflection. Consequently, weapons and contraband can successfully be hidden under a thick leather garment. Also, since glass and hard plastics will be detected; credit cards, women's cosmetics, etc., will be detected resulting in many false-positive detections. However, the guiding light beam will provide the officer with information on the location of the signal from which the officer may infer a significance of threat.

7.2 Walk-Through Metal Object Detector

The walk-through metal detector (WTMD) is a commonly used device for detecting metal weapons and contraband items. These devices are usually transportable; they can be moved by two people to different locations. WTMDs are used in close-proximity situations. Since most weapons are or contain significant metal, WTMDs can be used as the primary security screening tool in most situations,

35

such as courthouses, VIP security, school security, inmate visitation, etc. Some WTMDs are made to break down and transport in a van or trunk of a large car. Temperature and humidity affect the electronics, so outdoor applications, unless otherwise indicated by the manufacturer, should be avoided. WTMDs are available from many manufacturers and range in price from around $2000 to $10 000. They are presently the least expensive of walk-through type security screening devices.

7.2.1 Theory of Operation

WTMDs are metal detectors that use interaction of the time-varying magnetic field they produce with nearby objects for finding metal objects (see fig. 15). This interaction results in the generation of an electrical current in the object, and this process of current generation is how the WTMD detects a metal object. In fact, the WTMD can detect the presence of an object comprised of any electrically conductive or magnetizable material; the material does not necessarily have to be metallic but most electrically conductive or magnetizable objects are metallic (see reference 6 listed in section 9, which provides information on the operation of walk-through metal detectors). However, in most cases, the detection signal is too small to detect if the object is not a metal. The human body is also conductive, although not as conductive as a metal; but because of its size, the detection signal from the human body may be larger than the detection signal from certain small metal objects. WTMDs are frequently and incorrectly called magnetometers.

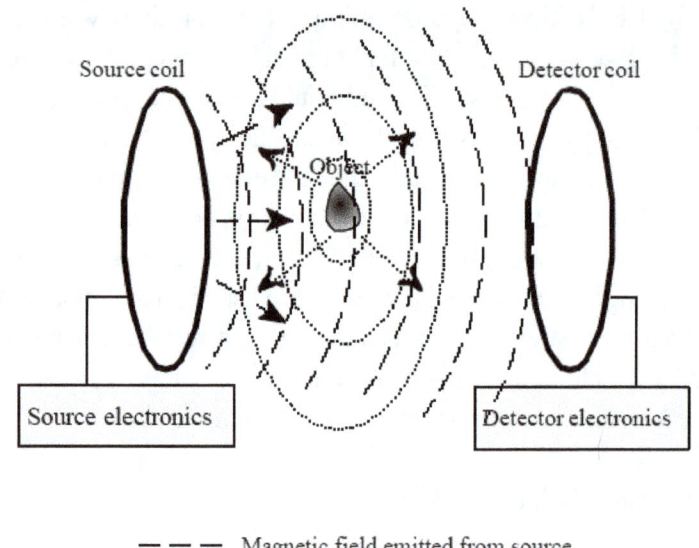

- - - Magnetic field emitted from source
.... Magnetic field emitted from object

Figure 15. Diagram of a metal detector with an object inside the detection space

7.2.2 Considerations for Use

The detection capability of WTMDs are limited to the size of metal objects that can be found on a person because of the interference caused by the person. Also, these devices primarily detect only metal objects. Unless the WTMD consists of multiple detectors (a zoned system), it will not provide any information on the location of the detected object. Even in the zoned systems, however, the location information is coarse.

7.3 Hand-Held Metal Object Detector

The hand-held metal detector (HHMD) is a commonly used device for detecting metal weapons and contraband items. These devices are light-weight and are used in close-proximity situations. HHMDs can be used to search for objects concealed on the body and, with some HHMDs, in body cavities. HHMDs can also be used to find metal objects in the yard of a correctional facility or in the quarters of an inmate. They are lightweight, can be easily carried, are low cost (range in price from around $200 to $500), easy to use, and have many commercial sources.

7.3.1 Theory of Operation

HHMDs are metal detectors that use the interaction of the time-varying magnetic field they produce with nearby objects for finding metal objects. The theory of operation of the HHMD is identical to the WTMD described in section 7.2.1. See reference 2 listed in section 9, which provides information on the operation of hand-held metal detectors.

7.3.2 Considerations for Use

HHMDs are used in close proximity situations. In fact, the hand-held metal detector must be held within a few inches of a metal object if the object is to be detected. The performance of many (at the time of this writing) metal detectors varies on a daily basis and must be accommodated by frequent adjustment, if provided. This variation in performance is not a limitation of the technology but of the quality control used to fabricate the HHMD. The recent revision in the National Institute of Justice standards takes steps to improve the performance of these devices. The HHMD is basically a metal detector and cannot be used to find weapons or contraband items made of other materials.

7.4 Magnetic Imaging Portal

This is a walk-through type CWCIDS that will use a set of small-sized closely-spaced antennae located around the perimeter of a portal or doorway. An image of the objects within the portal will be obtained as the objects move through the portal. This type of CWCIDS, depending on speed, could be used as a primary security screening tool. This CWCIDS is still under development and only a reduced-scale version has been made which uses several receivers and only one transmitter. The spatial resolution of this prototype system is presently 5 cm. Consequently, the image of a handgun would not be precise but it would be discernible. A video camera image is overlayed on the magnetic image to assist the operator in locating the object on the person. See reference 9 listed in section 9.

7.4.1 Theory of Operation

The time-varying magnetic field generated from each transmitter antenna interacts with objects within the detection space. That interaction, just like conventional hand-held and walk-through metal detectors, is based on the magnetic permeability and electrical conductivity of the object. The interaction of the generated magnetic field is detected at each receiver antenna. The metal objects in the target space are imaged by acquiring the signals for every receiver antenna and for each transmitter antenna. To obtain the data, one transmitter is turned on and each receiver acquires a signal. Then the next transmitter is turned on and each receiver acquires a new signal. This process continues until all transmitters along the periphery of the portal have had a chance to illuminate the detection space and each receiver has acquired a signal. To simplify design, the transmitter and receiver antennae are one and the same, and a computer-activated switch controls whether the antenna acts as a transmitter or a receiver. Therefore, each antenna is connected to its own transceiver (transmitter and receiver) circuit. Data is collected from each receiver during illumination by each transmitter. After all the data has been acquired, the image is constructed using a mathematical process called an inverse solutions algorithm. This image reconstruction process is similar to that used in computer-aided tomography and magnetic resonance imaging.

7.4.2 Considerations for Use

Image acquisition time may be slow to achieve the required spatial resolution over the required volume. However, to enhance image acquisition speed, an automatic image refinement algorithm is being investigated that will take successively higher resolution images only of those areas that exhibit detectable objects. This process may inadvertently reduce the spatial resolution required to find smaller objects during the first pass that may be of interest for certain LEC applications. Furthermore, the solution to inverse problems are frequently poor. A poor solution means poor image quality and, consequently, reduced detectability.

7.5 MRI Body Cavity Imager

The body cavity imager uses magnetic resonance imaging (MRI) techniques or, more accurately, nuclear magnetic resonance imaging techniques. This is the same technology used in medical MRI systems. Medical MRI systems are large and require the person being examined to lay on a narrow table that is inserted into the MRI system. However, reduction in the size and complexity of an MRI system is possible. An MRI system can find objects hidden deep within the body and could be used at high-security correctional facilities as a tertiary screening tool where conventional detection methods have not been able to resolve an alarm or if someone is suspected of ingesting contraband. See reference 10 listed in section 9 for a more detailed description of MRI.

7.5.1 Theory of Operation

MRI works by exposing the person to a large magnetic field pulse and then using a pulse of high-frequency microwave energy to probe the interaction of the magnetic field with the body. Specifically, the magnetic field pulse interacts with the nucleus of atoms and the microwave pulse is a probe that is used to examine this interaction. Not all atoms are MRI active. For an atom to be MRI active requires that the nucleus of the atom have either an odd number of protons, neutrons, or both (see ref. 10 listed in sec. 9). The frequency of the microwave probe is selected so that the probe only examines the interaction of a specific type of atom (such as the hydrogen atom) with the magnetic field. Since nuclei from different atoms behave differently when exposed to a pulsed magnetic field, MRI can be used to distinguish between different atoms and, consequently, different materials. Furthermore, the intensity of the MRI signal is dependent on the number of atoms of the given type. Therefore, an MRI system can be used by a trained operator to look for objects in a body cavity by looking for anomalies in the image. For example, assume the MRI system is tuned to look for the hydrogen atoms of water (MRI systems are typically tuned to look for protons, which are the nuclei of hydrogen atoms). If a body cavity should typically contain food or liquids (like the digestive system) and a weapon or contraband item is inside the cavity, the image from the MRI system will show a void in the cavity. This void in the MRI image is a result of the concealed item displacing the water containing materials.

7.5.2 Considerations for Use

MRI systems are large, expensive, may require water cooling, and require tens of amperes of ac power. However, research is being devoted to develop a transportable system that can operate in a large truck. Medical MRI images are typically interpreted by trained professionals, and radiologists, who are medical doctors. Consequently, the cost of operating the MRI systems may be high. Also, the large pulsed magnetic fields prevent MRI systems from being used on people with a personal medical electronic device, such as a pacemaker, cardiac defibrillator, infusion pump, etc. Voids in the MRI image can also be caused by air pockets, and this will result in false-positive signals.

7.6 Gradiometer Metal Detector

The gradiometer metal detector is a passive system and has been deployed in tests as a permanently installed part of a secure entry system for courthouses. In this scenario, a person must walk into a controlled area that is monitored via closed-circuit television cameras. The person removes metal objects until the alarms from the metal detector are resolved. The gradiometer system can be used as a primary security screening tool at locations, such as courthouses, where the primary threat items are conventional metal weapons. Because the gradiometer system is passive, it will not affect the function of personal medical electronic devices. Also, the system responds to moving ferromagnetic metal objects so that placing the system near stationary steel objects will not affect its operation. See reference 11 listed in section 9 for more information.

7.6.1 Theory of Operation

The gradiometer metal detector system is a walk-through type device that uses a series of vertically arranged gradiometers located on either side of its portal. A gradiometer consists of two magnetometers connected electrically in what is called differential mode. The gradiometer responds to changes in the local magnetic field of the earth caused by a moving ferromagnetic object. The differential mode connection is required to reduce the effects of normal background fluctuations that would otherwise cause false alarms. The gradiometer portal is very similar to a zoned walk-through metal detector. Each gradiometer pair responds to the presence of the ferromagnetic object and based on the magnitude of these interactions, the system displays the location of the metal object within the portal.

7.6.2 Considerations for Use

The spatial resolution and, consequently the smallest object that can be detected, is dependent on the number of gradiometers on either side of the portal. Increasing the number of gradiometers increases the cost of the system. The present design does not permit finding small objects such as handcuff keys, razor blades, etc. The gradiometer system requires that the target objects be ferromagnetic. Some metal weapons are not constructed of ferromagnetic metals and will go undetected. Metals such as, copper, brass, lead, aluminum, and some stainless steels are non-ferromagnetic. Furthermore, deployment as a permanent component in an integrated secure entry system may not be practical for most cases. Moreover, it may be necessary to deploy these units in a permanent installation because of the possibility of vibration- or movement-induced errors which would cause false-positives. These vibrations and movements may be caused by large nearby trucks, vibrating equipment, wind, etc. It may be possible to reduce the effects of movement and vibration by using three-axis accelerometers to measure the change in position of the magnetometers and, consequently, compensate the output of the magnetometers for any vibration or movement. This additional circuitry would increase system complexity and cost.

7.7 Gradiometer Metal Object Locator

The locator is a gradiometer-based device that is intended to be light-weight, portable, mobile, easy to use, and inexpensive. The locator is based on a military design for use in maritime applications. The locator is being designed to use less costly components than its military predecessor. It is intended to be carried by LEC officers and/or mounted on their vehicles. The metal object locator can be used to track persons carrying metal weapons or other large ferromagnetic metal objects. It can be used to track or locate items close to the locator or a few meters away. If mounted on a police cruiser, the locator can allow the officer to determine if anyone approaching the cruiser is carrying a large ferromagnetic object, such as a handgun. The locator is a passive device and, therefore, has no exposure concerns associated with it. See references 12 and 13 listed in section 9 for more information.

7.7.1 Theory of Operation

The metal object locator uses a gradiometer to locate the position of ferromagnetic metal objects. The gradiometer contains four three-axis magnetometers (see ref. 14 listed in sec. 9). One of the three axis magnetometers is used as a reference. The other three three-axis magnetometers (or sensor magnetometers) are located equidistant from each other and from the centrally located reference gradiometer. Each sensor magnetometer is contained within a set of uniquely designed coils that is used to null (zero) the background (Earth) magnetic field, greatly improving the dynamic range of the gradiometer system compared to other compensation methods. Nulling the background magnetic field is accomplished by applying an electrical current to the sensor magnetometer coils. This electrical current is controlled by the reference magnetometer such that, in the presence of a uniform magnetic field, the output of the sensor magnetometers is zero. The advantage of this design is the large increase in dynamic range and, consequently, the ability to locate and track ferromagnetic objects, compared to other gradiometer systems.

7.7.2 Considerations for Use

Only ferromagnetic objects can be located and tracked. However, most objects that are a threat to an officer, such as knives and firearms, contain ferromagnetic metals. The size of an object that can be tracked is dependent on the distance between the object and the locator. Consequently, these devices would not be able to locate and track small items that are a threat to security in a correctional facility, such as handcuff keys, razor blades, etc., from more than 1 m. Although the detection of a moving object is not affected by ferromagnetic objects that are stationary relative to the gradiometer, large ferromagnetic objects will distort the magnetic field near the gradiometer and possibly cause incorrect object distances. However, the effects of some large objects can be compensated, and this allows the gradiometer to be attached to a motor vehicle and still be capable of locating and tracking a ferromagnetic object. Car vibrations (caused by opening and closing doors, motor-induced low-frequency suspension vibrations) will affect gradiometer performance.

7.8 Microwave Holographic Imager

The microwave holographic imager is a portal-type device where the person being searched is scanned by microwave energy. To obtain the image, a column containing a set of vertically-arranged emitter and detector pairs is rotated around the stationary person. The emitter radiates continuous-wave energy. The detected signal is used to accurately construct an image of the surface of the person. This system has been evaluated for operator ease-of-use at several airports. See reference 15 for more information.

7.8.1 Theory of Operation

Holographic imaging is based on the interference (see sec. 5.4.4) of two beams of electromagnetic waves: one beam is called the reference beam and the other the object beam. The object beam, because it reflects off the target field, contains information on the target. Specifically, this target information is the distance from the object to the source and the reflectivity of the target. The holographic image is the result of the addition of the reference beam with the target beam. Holographic images are conventionally captured and stored on film and subsequently displayed by illuminating the film with light. In this application, however, the image is captured by microwave detectors and stored as data in a computer. The image is then displayed on a computer monitor or other display device. For an introduction on holography, see reference 16 listed in section 9 or a similar text.

The spatial resolution of a holographic image is dependent on the wavelength of the emitted radiation; the shorter the wavelength, the higher the spatial resolution. The time required to make a holographic image is a signal-to-noise issue (see sec. 5.3.2.3) and depends on the power in the reference beam and in the reflected target beam. The target must be stationary while the image is being acquired or else the image will be distorted. Furthermore, microwave radiation readily penetrates most clothing material but not the human body. Therefore, all body surfaces must be imaged to determine if an object is hidden underneath clothing. Imaging of different body surfaces is accomplished by revolving the microwave emitters and detectors around the person or, equivalently, by rotating the person within a stationary array of emitters and detectors.

The microwave detectors presently available for use in microwave holographic imaging systems are fairly sensitive and, therefore, do not require significant microwave power. The microwave holographic imaging system emits power at a level well below that which is considered unsafe.

7.8.2 Considerations for Use

Microwave radiation is absorbed by the human body. Therefore, objects hidden in body cavities would not be found. In addition, the images acquired from the present holographic system contain anatomical detail. Therefore, for some applications, the image detail would have to be reduced or the data acquired so that it did not contain such information. However, these are not limitations that cannot be overcome with special algorithms. However, as mentioned in section 7.8.1, the image must be taken while the object is stationary. Therefore, it is necessary that the person being imaged remain still for the duration of the image acquisition time. Present acquisition time is a few seconds. There is concern with the imaging array rotating around an individual, especially a child or a claustrophobic.

7.9 Microwave Dielectrometer Imager

The microwave dielectrometer is based on measuring the dielectric constant (see sec. 5.4.2.1) of materials passing by a vertically arranged set of dielectrometers. The dielectrometer imager is a portal-type device that requires scanning the different surfaces of a person with microwave energy; this is similar to the system described in section 7.8, but uses a different method to collect and display information. The person remains stationary while the column of dielectrometers is rotated around the person.

7.9.1 Theory of Operation

Each dielectrometer in the portal consists of an emitter and detector pair. The detectors contain a specially designed narrow frequency, high-gain, three-dimensional antenna. The emitter circuit is designed to transmit a single cycle of microwave radiation. The detected signal is caused by objects that have electronic properties (see sec. 5.4.2.1) different from that of air. Specifically, the electronic properties are the dielectric permittivity and the electrical conductivity. For more detailed information on the interaction of electromagnetic waves with matter, see, for example, reference 17 listed in section 9. The detected signal contains amplitude information and delay information. The amplitude gives a measure of the material property values, and the delay gives information on the distance between the emitter and the object. This system is designed so that only anomalies or differences in the material property of the surrounding environment and human bodies are detected. Consequently, no anatomical information is acquired or contained in the image data. To present the image, however, requires that the objects be displayed on a wire frame representation of an average human. The height of the wire frame model is scaled by the location of a handlebar which is to be held shoulder height by the person being scanned.

7.9.2 Considerations for Use

Scanning, as with the CWCIDS described in section 7.8, takes several seconds. There is concern with the imaging array rotating around an individual, especially a child. Present spatial resolution is 5 cm (2 in), and this is limited by the dielectrometer size and the separation between dielectrometers. Presently, the dielectrometers used in the system are expensive and increasing the spatial resolution will increase the cost of the system.

7.10 X-ray Imager

The x-ray imager uses the same technology as medical x-ray imagers (see ref. 18 and 19 listed in sec. 9). The person being scanned stands near a panel while an x-ray source is scanned across the body. Each surface of the body to be imaged requires a separate scan.

7.10.1 Theory of Operation

X-rays are a form of electromagnetic energy. The x-rays used in these devices are of low energy and penetrate a few millimeters into the body. The interaction of x-rays with matter is complex and can lead to the production of electrons and other x-rays (see, for example, ref. 20 listed in sec. 9). Medical x-ray imagers rely on the absorption of incident x-rays for imaging. Weapon detection x-ray imaging systems, on the other hand, utilize an interaction called Compton scattering or backscattering. Frequently, these imaging systems are called backscatter imagers. The Compton effect is a quantum mechanical phenomenon. In Compton scattering, an x-ray photon interacts with an electron bound to an atom. (A photon is one quantum of electromagnetic energy.) In this interaction, the electron absorbs some of the incident x-ray energy and this absorbed energy is transferred to the kinetic (motional) energy of the electron. The energy of the x-ray photon that interacts with the electron is thus reduced by the amount transferred to the kinetic energy of the electron. This reduced energy x-ray photon is the Compton scattered x-ray photon used for imaging. For more information on Compton scattering, see, for example, reference 21 listed in section 9.

7.10.2 Considerations for Use

X-ray backscatter imaging has sufficient spatial resolution to identify concealed contraband and weapon items. These items do not have to be metallic; consequently, drugs, chemicals, etc., can be found on a person. However, these x-ray systems do not have the penetration capability to find objects hidden within body cavities or concealed otherwise under heavy flesh. Each surface of the body that may contain a concealed object must be imaged. The present commercially-available systems are sufficiently fast, a few seconds per scan and up to four scans per person, to be used as secondary screening devices in high-throughput applications. However, the x-ray images will raise privacy issues since they contain detailed anatomical information. There has been concern expressed whether having the detailed image data violates an individual's privacy even if that detail is not displayed. Consequently, the images or imagers may have to be altered. Altering the image will, more than likely, reduce image quality and clarity, and therefore, the ability to identify small contraband and weapon items. There may also be a safety concern because x-ray radiation is ionizing. However, these x-ray systems emit low dosages, much below that which the USFDA believes is a threat to health. However, the USFDA does not have an official position on the safety of these devices.

7.11 Microwave Radar Imager

The present implementation of the microwave radar imager is as a through-the-wall people finder that uses a frequency-modulated cw source (see sec. 5.3). However, by reducing the wavelength so that spatial resolution is improved (see sec. 5.4), the radar imager can also be used to image concealed objects. The microwave radar imager is a small, light-weight device that can be deployed at any location and be operated remotely. The microwave radar imager uses electromagnetic radiation in the 20 GHz to 100 GHz range. For more details, see reference 22 listed in section 9.

7.11.1 Theory of Operation

The image is formed from reflections of the microwave energy by objects within the target space of the imager. Radar (an acronym for radio detection and ranging) is used to determine the motion of the reflecting object by detecting the Doppler-frequency shift in the reflected (or return) signal. This shift is the result of the object moving away from or closer to the source of microwave energy. If the object is moving away, the return signal has a longer wavelength (lower frequency); if the object is moving toward the source, the return signal has a shorter wavelength (higher frequency). The equations describing the Doppler-frequency shift are simple and, therefore, an accurate measurement of the Doppler-frequency shift will provide an accurate measurement of the motion of the object.

To obtain distance or range information, the continuous-wave source must be modulated. A common modulation method that works is frequency modulation. A frequency modulated source can be viewed as a cw source where the frequency of the emitted power changes with time. Range information from a frequency-modulated (FM) cw radar system is obtained in the following way (see fig. 16). The source illuminates the target space with a FM cw signal transmitted by an antenna. The reflected signal is subsequently collected by the same antenna. Some of the output of the source enters the mixer via the circulator. The source is typically called the local oscillator (LO). Similarly, the reflected signal power enters the mixer via the circulator. The two signals, the incident and the reflected signals, are then combined in the mixer in a way that can be used to compute the distance between the source and the reflecting object. The mixer output is typically called the intermediate frequency (IF) signal. For the purpose of this discussion, the IF signal provided by the mixer has a

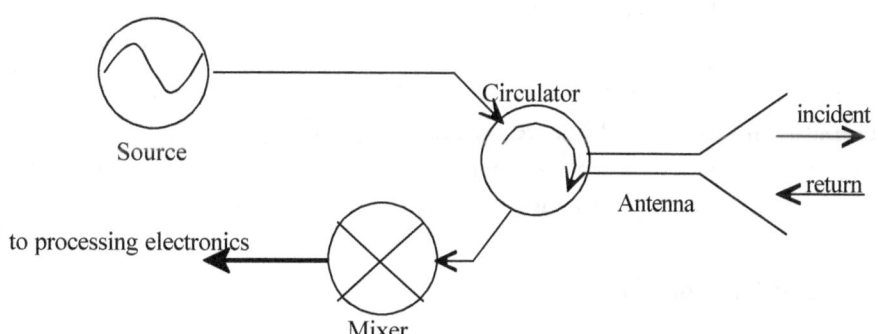

Figure 16. Diagram of an implementation of a cw-Doppler radar system

frequency that is the set by the difference between the frequency of the LO and the frequency of the reflected signals. If the LO was not frequency modulated, the signal would be very difficult to observe or acquire. The frequency of the IF signal provides information on the range to the reflecting object, and the magnitude of the IF signal provides an indication of the size of the reflecting object.

7.11.2 Considerations for Use

The spatial resolution of the microwave radar imager is dependent on the microwave wavelength (or frequency). For example, a 55 GHz system will provide 5 cm (2 in) spatial resolution. The smaller the wavelength, the greater the spatial resolution. However, the smaller the wavelength, the more likely the radar energy will be absorbed by intervening materials, such as brick walls. Consequently, the spatial resolution required to detect weapons at a distance may preclude through-the-wall applications. The image acquisition time is dependent on the area to be imaged. However, for most applications (distances less than 10 m away, horizontal scan of less than 2 m, and a 1 m vertical scan) the image scan time should be less than a couple of seconds.

7.12 Pulse Radar/Swept Frequency Detector

The system being developed uses a pulse radar to determine the range to the object and then uses a swept frequency illumination of the object to obtain information on the object. Both hand-held and portable stationary-use units are under development.

7.12.1 Theory of Operation

A pulse of microwave or radio-frequency energy is used to illuminate the target space and the reflected signal provides information on range. For pulse radar, acquiring range information is achieved by measuring the time interval between the emitted illumination pulse and the return pulse. After the object position and range have been determined with the pulse radar subsystem, the object is illuminated by a swept frequency source. The swept frequency return signal from the object is then analyzed to determine if the reflecting object is a threat item. In particular, the resonance of the reflecting object is used to extract information about the object, thus providing a signature for the object. The object's electromagnetic signature is then compared to that of known handgun signatures, and an alarm is automatically activated if the signatures match; there is no operator interpretation of an image.

7.12.2 Considerations for Use

The system does not provide an image but an indication of whether or not a threat item is present in the target space. The ability to determine the existence of a threat item requires that the system store these signatures in a data base. Although storing and sorting through frequency signatures (or spectra) of threat items is not as memory and processor intensive as image recognition, the same problems still apply (see sec. 2.1.2). Consequently, there may be delays while the computer searches the database for possible matches. As the threat items change, the data base must be updated to accommodate these new threats.

7.13 Broadband/Noise Pulse Millimeter-Wave/Terahertz-Wave Imager

This system is a pulse imaging system that uses either broadband or noise pulses. It is intended to be a car-portable system with a stand-off scanning distance of 7 m and an image refresh rate of 10 Hz (10 images per second) or more, thereby providing real-time imaging capability.

7.13.1 Theory of Operation

A very short duration pulse or a noise pulse is used to illuminate a target space. Objects in the target space reflect the incident signal and this reflected energy allows imaging of objects within the target space. This is similar to the way a conventional camera works except, in this case, the illumination source is the pulse source, not the sun, and the detection or imaging is done with special detectors and not a photographic film. However, the general concepts are the same. As with a photographic image, distance to objects and size of objects are inferred by the observer.

There are two potential methods for detection of the reflected pulse energy that are being explored.

One is based on antenna coupled microbolometer arrays and the other on electrooptic properties of materials. Both methods are being investigated because both have the potential for providing real-time imaging capability. The detailed description of these techniques is beyond the scope of this Guide. For more information, see references 23 and 24 listed in section 9.

Broadband or noise pulses are used to avoid adverse imaging effects, such as interference (see sec. 5.4.4), that occur when using a monochromatic coherent illumination source. Interference can cause the image of a flat reflecting surface to exhibit bright and dark regions that are dependent on the angle of illumination. Because a broadband or noise pulse source produces energy comprised of many frequency components (see sec. 5.3.2.2), the effects of interference are removed. For example, interference is not experienced in visible photography which uses a broadband light source, the sun, for illumination.

7.13.2 Considerations for Use

As with any active system, the target space must be illuminated with sufficient energy to observe a reflected signal; this is a signal-to-noise issue (see sec. 5.3.2.3). Furthermore, there is a limit to the amount of average power that an individual can be exposed to and this is described in reference 25 listed in section 9. Consequently, there is a trade-off between safety issues and signal quality issues. A pulse source can provide the illumination energy required for quality images without exceeding the safe exposure limits; this is typically not the case for a continuous wave illumination system. The system may be expensive and this is dependent on the cost of the components used for the chosen detection method.

7.14 Millimeter-Wave Radar Detector

The microwave radar detector is intended to be a hand-held device that has an operating range of approximately 1 m to 7 m. The radar detector is a frequency-modulated cw radar and consists of a radar energy emitter and detector. However, in this case, the emitted radar energy is scanned horizontally by the unit and vertically by the operator. The emitted frequency is centered around 95 GHz and the horizontal scan is about ± 5•. The target image acquisition time is approximately 1 s.

7.14.1 Theory of Operation

The radar detector uses the energy reflected from objects in the target field to generate an image. The distance between the object and the detector can be obtained because of the emitter and sensor design; namely, the emitter provides a frequency-modulated cw output and the sensor contains a millimeter-wave mixer that mixes the reflected signal and a coherent (see sec. 5.3.1) reference signal. The output of the mixer is dependent on the magnitude of the reflected signal and the phase or frequency relationship (see sec. 5.3.1) between the reflected and reference signals. An image is actually obtained with this CWCIDS; therefore, image recognition hardware and/or software is required (see sec. 2.1.1).

47

To improve image recognition, the image is enhanced algorithmically.

7.14.2 Considerations for Use

The detection ability of this CWCIDS is dependent on the operating wavelength and the wavelength dependent object properties (see sec. 5.4). This system is basically a FM cw radar and diffraction will limit spatial resolution and object recognition. The robustness of the image recognition algorithms will also affect detection capability.

7.15 Electromagnetic Pulse Detector

This system is similar to that described in section 7.12 in that both rely on the electromagnetic properties of target objects to provide a unique signature for object identification. Both pulse and swept frequency illumination are being examined. The final system will be a field-deployable unit. For more information see reference 26 listed in section 9.

7.15.1 Theory of Operation

The target space is illuminated with either a pulse or swept frequency source. The signal reflected by objects in the target space provides an electromagnetic signature, a unique spectrum, for that object. The object signatures are then compared to known signatures to determine whether or not objects in the target space are threat items (this is similar to that described in sec. 7.12). The person carrying the object will also exhibit a unique electromagnetic signature. To recover the signature from the object requires that the signature of the person be subtracted from the composite person-object signature.

7.15.2 Considerations for Use

The method for assessing whether or not an object in the target space is a threat item involves comparing measured spectra to known spectra. This requires a local data base containing stored spectra. Moreover, the measured spectra will depend on the orientation of the target objects relative to the illumination source. Consequently, the data base must also contain the spectra for the object for all its unique orientations. Moreover, this method is dependent on having an average human signature. Based on the diversity of size, shape, and mass distribution of humans, it may be very difficult to obtain an average human signature.

7.16 Millimeter-Wave Imager

There are a variety of different millimeter-wave (mm-wave) imagers being developed for concealed weapon detection applications, see references 27 to 29. The difference in these devices is in the detection of the mm-wave energy. These devices are presently in the development stage and none have been deployed or tested in actual use.

7.16.1 Theory of Operation

As mentioned in section 5.1.2, bodies at temperatures above absolute zero will emit radiation and the wavelength of the radiation peak is dependent on the temperature of the body. The total power emitted from the body is dependent on the size and emissivity of the body. Passive mm-wave imaging is based on the ability to detect the mm-wave energy emitted by people relative to that emitted by a weapon. These detection systems, like thermal imaging (see sec. 7.17), require the ability to differentiate between temperatures of adjacent areas within the target area. The operation of a passive mm-wave imager, or a thermal imager, can be compared to the operation of a camera. The light for a mm-wave imager is the mm-wave energy and the film of a camera is the detector array in a mm-wave imager. The differences among the systems being explored for concealed weapon detection is in the mode of detection. The details of these differences are beyond the scope of this guide; please see references 27 to 29 listed in section 9.

7.16.2 Considerations for Use

The mm-wave imagers, because of the detector technology and requirement to have almost-real-time imaging, do not have the temperature sensitivity of thermal (infrared) imagers. Present systems, at best, have a 1 • C temperature sensitivity and require several seconds to acquire an image under the best of conditions. Due to this low temperature sensitivity, concealed weapons or contraband that have been in contact with the body, and are at body temperature, will not be detected by present passive mm-wave imagers. However, with improved detector responsivity, it may be possible to develop an almost-real-time passive mm-wave imager. However, the effect of a weapon-to-body temperature difference will still be an issue. Furthermore, the person being scanned for a concealed object must be stationary while the image is being acquired or the image will become blurred and indecipherable.

7.17 Infrared Imager

Infrared imagers are commonly used for a variety of night-vision applications for seeing vehicles and people. See reference 30 for a description of infrared imagers.

7.17.1 Theory of Operation

As mentioned in section 5.1.2, bodies at temperatures above absolute zero will emit radiation and the wavelength of the radiation peak is dependent on the temperature of the body, and the total power emitted from the body is dependent on the size and emissivity of the body. Most thermal imagers have been designed to have a peak sensitivity near the peak emission wavelength of humans, namely around 10 μm (see fig. 4). Also, these thermal imagers have better than 0.1 • C temperature sensitivity, which allows the images to display detailed features, such as the facial features of people.

7.17.2 Considerations for Use

Infrared radiation emitted by people is absorbed by clothing. This absorbed radiation heats the clothing and is then re-emitted by the clothing. Consequently, the image of a concealed weapon will be blurred, at best, assuming the clothing is tight and stationary. For normally loose clothing, the emitted infrared radiation will be spread over a larger clothing area thereby significantly decreasing the ability to image a weapon. The difficulty in observing an infrared signal of a concealed weapon becomes worse as the weapon temperature approaches that of the body.

7.18 Hybrid Millimeter-Wave and Infrared Imager

Hybrid millimeter-wave and infrared imagers are systems that employ both mm-wave and infrared imaging techniques (see secs. 7.16 and 7.17). The images from these two separate imaging subsystems are brought together algorithmically in what is called a fusion process. The fusion of the mm-wave and infrared images results in the fused image. See reference 31 for a brief discussion of this method.

7.18.1 Theory of Operation

The theory of operation of the separate imaging systems was described in sections 7.16 and 7.17. The fusion process requires that the images be aligned properly. Before alignment, each image is filtered to remove extraneous or noisy data and enhanced to augment certain image features. The enhancement facilitates subsequent image alignment.

7.18.2 Considerations for Use

The fused data is the result of infrared and mm-wave images. If the infrared image cannot contain information on the concealed item, it will provide no useful information. In most situations, clothing will prevent acquisition of any information on a concealed weapon. Consequently, the fused image provides no further information on the concealed weapon than that provided by the mm-wave imager. Mm-wave images take a few seconds to acquire and during this time the person must be stationary. The fused image may exhibit no more than a mm-wave image of the concealed weapon with a high-resolution image of the surface of the clothing. However, the infrared image does facilitate location of human subjects, on which an object may be hidden, and this may accelerate the subsequent process of detecting a weapon on the subject.

8. SUGGESTIONS AND RECOMMENDATIONS FOR PERFORMANCE STANDARDS

The purpose of this section is to provide general ideas for developing performance standards for a CWCIDS. For two of the technologies described in section 7, namely the walk-through (sec. 7.2) and hand-held (sec. 7.3) metal detectors, the National Institute of Justice (NIJ) already has standards (see refs. 32 and 33 listed in sec. 9).

8.1 Revised NIJ Standards for Hand-held (HH) and Walk-through (WT) Metal Detectors

The original NIJ standards were revised and expanded to accommodate requirements expressed by the law enforcement and corrections community. These new requirements not only included detection performance improvements but also new requirements for system performance including the operator interface and/or controls, more realistic test objects, environmental tolerance, electromagnetic compatibility, quality control and assurance, safety, and operator instructional and technical repair documentation. Many of these new requirements can be used verbatim or as a template for consistency for future standards for concealed weapon and contraband imaging and detection systems.

8.2 Detection/Imaging Performance Requirements and Specifications

The most important requirements will be for the detector/imager performance. These requirements should be written such that they are dependent on the LEC application and not on the system or technology used for the given application. Furthermore, more than one technology may be applied to a given LEC application. Consequently, the LEC community must have a clear idea of what their requirements are for a given application before attempting to write a standard. By having an application-dependent standard, it is possible for more than one technology to be applied to and to compete for the LEC given application. For example, WT metal detectors can be manufactured by the technology described in sections 7.2 and 7.4. It is beneficial to the LEC community to have more than one technology or adaptation of a given technology used for a given LEC application because this redundancy generates competition which results in improvements to the CWCIDS technologies and to CWCIDS cost reductions.

It may also be possible to use one technology for more than one LEC application. Therefore, developing standards based on technology alone may not be productive and may actually limit the efficacy of a CWCIDS and, consequently, that of the LEC agencies. For example, the NIJ standards for HH and WT metal detectors are based on the same technology but are written for very different applications. A common performance standard for both applications would not ensure the desired performance for either a HH or WT metal detector. (The HH metal detector standard is written with the application of finding metal objects using a fast close proximity search technique whereas the WT metal detector standard is written for the application of finding metal objects passing through a portal-type device.)

51

8.3 Other Performance Requirements

Many of the system performance requirements should be the same for any detection/imaging system that is intended to be used by the law enforcement and corrections community. For example, documentation, quality control and assurance, electromagnetic compatibility, and environmental tolerance should be similar if not identical to that described in the revised NIJ standards for hand-held and walk-through metal detectors. These requirements are somewhat generic in nature and have been presented as such in the revised NIJ metal detector standards.

Safety requirements can be divided between electrical, mechanical, chemical, and radiation exposure. Exposure requirements will, of course, be different for different types of CWCIDSs because of the variety of sources used for illuminating the target space. There is the concern for both operator and general public safety, and this will also vary among the CWCIDSs because of source differences. However, all CWCIDSs will have to comply with safe operating requirements including absence of sharp edges, loose covers and cowlings, exposed wires, etc. These issues are treated in the revised NIJ standards for HH and WT metal detectors. Passive systems do not actively emit energy and, therefore, will not have exposure issues.

The operator interface and controls will be dependent on the type of system being used. However, the requirements in the revised NIJ HH and WT metal detector standards can provide a starting point for these requirements.

9. REFERENCES

1. J.D. Kraus and K.R. Carver, *Electromagnetics, Second Edition*, McGraw-Hill Book Company, New York, 1973.

2. E.M. Purcell, *Electricity and Magnetism, Second Edition*, McGraw-Hill Book Company, New York, 1985.

3. S. Ramo, J.R. Whinnery, and T. Van Duzer, *Fields and Waves in Communication Electronics, Second Edition*, John Wiley & Sons, New York, 1984.

4. F.A. Jenkins and H.E. White, *Fundamentals of Optics, Fourth Edition*, McGraw-Hill Book Company, 1976.

5. Max Born and Emil Wolf, *Principles of Optics, Electromagnetic Theory of Propagation, Interference and Diffraction of Light, Sixth Edition*, Pergamon Press, New York, 1983.

6. N.G. Paulter, *Users' Guide for Hand-Held and Walk-Through Metal Detectors*, NIJ Guide 600–00, NCJ 184433, Office of Science and Technology, U.S. Department of Justice, Washington, DC 20531, January 2001.

7. H.F. Henry, *Fundamentals of Radiation Protection*, Wiley-Interscience, New York, 1969.

8. F. Felber, N. Wild, S. Nunan, D. Breuner, and F. Doft, "Handheld ultrasound concealed-weapons detector," Proceedings of the SPIE, The International Society for Optical Engineering, *Conference on Enforcement and Security Technologies*, Vol. 3575, pp. 89 to 98, Boston, MA, November, 1998. ("SPIE" is the acronym for the Society of Photo-optical Instrumentation Engineers which is the former name of the International Society for Optical Engineering. The International Society for Optical Engineering continues to use the acronym "SPIE.")

9. B. Zollars, B. Sallee, M. Durrett, C. Cruce, and W. Hallidy, "Concealed weapons detection using low-frequency magnetic imaging," Proceedings of the SPIE, The International Society for Optical Engineering, *Conference on Surveillance and Assessment Technologies for Law Enforcement*, Vol. 2935, pp.108 to 119, Boston, MA, November 1996.

10. R.C. Smith and R.C. Lange, *Understanding Magnetic Resonant Imaging*, CRC Press, New York, 1997.

11. L.G. Roybal, P.M. Rice, and J.M. Manhardt, "A new approach for detecting and classifying concealed weapons," Proceedings of the SPIE, The International Society for Optical

Engineering, *Conference on Surveillance and Assessment Technologies for Law Enforcement*, Vol. 2935, pp. 95 to 107, Boston, MA, November 1996.

12.   G.I. Allen, P. Czipott, R. Matthews, and R.H. Koch, "Initial evaluation and follow on investigation of the Quantum Magnetics laboratory prototype, room temperature gradiometer for ordnance location," Proceedings of the SPIE, The International Society for Optical Engineering, *Conference on Information Systems for Navy Divers and Autonomous Vehicles Operating in Very Shallow Water and Surf Zone Regions*, Vol. 3711, pp. 103 to 112, Orlando, FL, April 1999.

13.   P.V. Czipott and M.D. Iwanowski, "Magnetic sensor technology for detecting mines, UXO, and other concealed security threats," Proceedings of the SPIE, The International Society for Optical Engineering, *Conference on Terrorism and Counter-terrorism Methods and Technologies*, pp. 67 to 76, Boston, MA, November 1996.

14.   R.H. Koch, G.A. Keefe, and G. Allen, "Room temperature three sensor magnetic field gradiometer," Review of Scientific Instruments, Vol. 67, pp. 230 to 235, January 1996.

15.   D.L. McMakin, D.M. Sheen, T.E. Hall, and R.H. Severtsen, "Cylindrical holographic radar camera," Proceedings of the SPIE, *Conference on Enforcement and Security Technologies*, Vol. 3575, pp. 75 to 88, Boston, MA, November, 1998.

16.   E. Hecht and A. Zajac, *Optics*, Addison-Wesley Publishing Company, Reading, MA, 1979.

17.   S. Ramo, J.R. Whinnery, and T. Van Duzer, *Fields and Waves in Communication Electronics, Second Edition*, John Wiley & Sons, New York, 1984.

18.   D.S. deMoulpied, P.J. Rothschild, and G. Smith, "X-ray BodySearch™ eliminates strip search in Montana prison," Proceedings of the SPIE, The International Society for Optical Engineering, *Conference on Enforcement and Security Technologies*, Vol. 3575, pp. 175 to 181, Boston, MA, November, 1998.

19.   S.W. Smith, "The SECURE personnel screening system: field trials and new developments," Proceedings of the SPIE, The International Society for Optical Engineering, *Conference on Human Detection and Positive Identification: Methods and Technologies*, Vol. 2932, pp. 121 to 125, Boston, MA, November, 1996.

20.   T.A. Delchar, *Physics in Medical Diagnosis*, Chapman & Hall, London, 1997.

21.   D. Halliday and R. Resnick, *Fundamentals of Physics*, John Wiley & Sons, New York, 1974.

22.   L.M. Frazier, "Surveillance through non-metallic walls," Proceedings of the SPIE, The International Society for Optical Engineering, *Conference on Enforcement and Security Technologies*, Vol. 3575, pp. 108 to 112, Boston, MA, November, 1998.

23.   N.G. Paulter, "Specific NIST projects in support of the NIJ Concealed Weapon Detection and Imaging Program," Proceedings of the SPIE, The International Society for Optical Engineering, *Conference on Enforcement and Security Technologies*, Vol. 3575, pp. 124 to 131, Boston, MA, November, 1998.

24.   S. Nolen, J. A. Koch, N.G. Paulter, C. D. Reintsema, E. N. Grossman, "Antenna-coupled niobium bolometers for mm-wave imaging arrays," Proceedings of the SPIE, The International Society for Optical Engineering, *Conference on Terahertz and Gigahertz Photonics*, Vol. 3795, Denver, CO, July 1999.

25.   IEEE C95.1-1991, *Standard for Safety Levels with Respect to Human Exposure to Radio Frequency Electromagnetic Fields, 3 kHz to 300 GHz*, Institute of Electrical and Electronic Engineers, New York, 1992.

26.   A.R. Hunt, R. D. Hogg, and W. Foreman, "Concealed weapons detection using electromagnetic resonance," Proceedings of the SPIE, The International Society for Optical Engineering, *Conference on Enforcement and Security Technologies*, Vol. 3575, pp. 62 to 67, Boston, MA, November, 1998.

27.   G.R. Huguenin, "Millimeter-wave video rate imagers," Proceedings of the SPIE, The International Society for Optical Engineering, *Conference on Passive Millimeter-wave Imaging Technology*, Vol. 3064, pp. 34 to 45, Orlando, FL, April, 1997

28.   A. Luukanen and V.-P. Viitanen, "Terahertz imaging system based on antenna-coupled microbolometers," Proceedings of the SPIE, The International Society for Optical Engineering, *Conference on Passive Millimeter-wave Imaging Technology II*, Vol. 3378, pp. 34 to 44, Orlando, FL, April 1998.

29.   F.J. Demma, N.C. Currie, D.D. Ferris, Jr., R.W. McMillan, and M.C. Wicks, Operations Other Than Warfare/Law Enforcement Sensor Technology Study, Rome Laboratory In-House Report RL-Tr-96-5, Rome, NY, 1996.

30.   P.W. Kruse and D.D. Skatrud, Editors, *Uncooled Infrared Imaging Arrays and Systems, in Semiconductors and Semimetals*, Volume 47, Academic Press, San Diego, CA, 1997.

31.   M.-A. Slamani, P.K. Varshney, R.M. Rao, and M.G. Alford, "An integrated platform for the enhancement of concealed weapon detection sensors," Proceedings of the SPIE, The

International Society for Optical Engineering, *Conference on Enforcement and Security Technologies*, Vol. 3575, pp. 68 to 78, Boston, MA, November, 1998.

32.   *Walk-Through Metal Detectors for Use in Concealed Weapon and Contraband Detection*, NIJ Standard–0601.01, NCJ 183471, prepared by Nicholas G. Paulter, Jr., National Institute of Standards and Technology, Gaithersburg, MD for the Office of Science and Technology, U.S. Department of Justice, Washington, DC 20531, September 2000.

33.   *Hand-Held Metal Detectors for Use in Concealed Weapon and Contraband Detection*, NIJ Standard–0602.01, NCJ 183470, prepared by Nicholas G. Paulter, Jr., National Institute of Standards and Technology, Gaithersburg, MD for the Office of Science and Technology, U.S. Department of Justice, Washington, DC 20531, September 2000.